THE AUTHORS

Pedro Lima, a scientific journalist specialising in prehistory and parietal art, wrote the text. His work has given him the opportunity to visit numerous decorated sites, among them Lascaux and Chauvet-Pont d'Arc.

Philippe Psaïla, photographer and videographer specialising in research, science and discovery, made the photographs and images inside the 3D model of the Chauvet-Pont d'Arc cave. He visited the original cave, and his pictures do justice to its incomparable beauty.

Guy Perazio created the 3D model used to make the pictures of cave art illustrating this work. He first entered the Chauvet-Pont d'Arc cave in 1997 to make the original topographic study and spent a total of 140 days there.

From the Same Authors
Pedro Lima and Philippe Psaïla wrote and photographed *The Many Metamophoses of Lascaux: The Artist's Studio from Prehistory to Today*, preface by Jean Clottes, published by Synops in 2012.

Cover photograph: Horse in the central alcove of the End Chamber panel, by Philippe Psaïla/Perazio.

ISBN 978-2-9542888-3-3

www.synops-editions.fr

Chauvet-Pont d'Arc

THE FIRST MASTERPIECE OF HUMANITY

REVEALED BY 3D

Text by **Pedro Lima**

Photographs by **Philippe Psaïla**

3D images by **Philippe Psaïla and Cabinet Perazio**

Preface: **Aurélie Filippetti**

Forward: **Pascal Terrasse**

Scientific Adviser: **Benjamin Sadier**

Translated from the French by **Venetia Bell**

HOW DO I ACCESS MULTIMEDIA CONTENT?

If you have a computer

Go to:

www.thefirstmasterpiece.com

Select "multimedia access"

www.thefirstmasterpiece.com

And follow the instructions

Or go directly to:

www.thefirstmasterpiece.com/help.html

An expanded and dynamic work

In the months to come, we will add new content to what's already online. For updates and news about the Chauvet-Pont d'Arc cave, subscribe to our newsletter by flashing the cover or go directly to www.thefirstmasterpiece.com.

SYNOPS

With *The First Masterpiece of Humanity*, Éditions Synops places books and printed matter at the centre of digital devices to prolong and enrich the reading experience.
www.synops-editions.fr

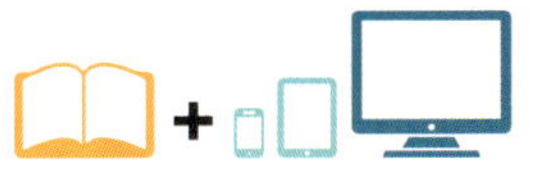

INSTRUCTIONS FOR USE

You have a mobile

(smartphone, tablet)

Download and install
the free SYNAPPS application at Apple Store, Google Play and *www.thefirstmasterpiece.com*

Select the content you want in the menu that appears and make the experience of the Chauvet-Pont d'Arc cave last longer!

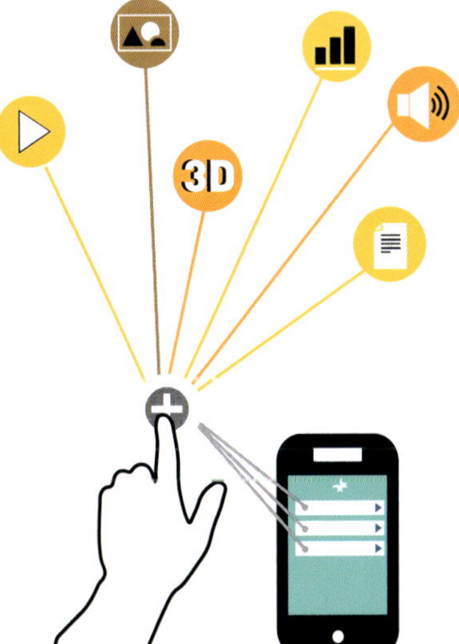

Identify + "flash"
the pages with this pictogram

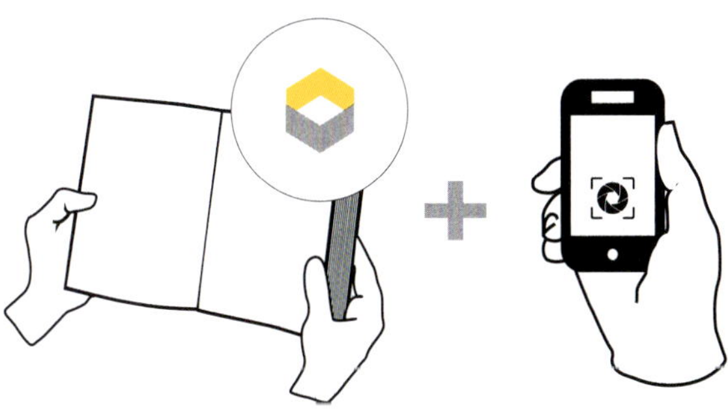

Flash the cover

(Discovery)

For a sample of the different kinds of media associated with this work.

•

PLAN OF THE CHAUVET-PONT D'ARC CAVE

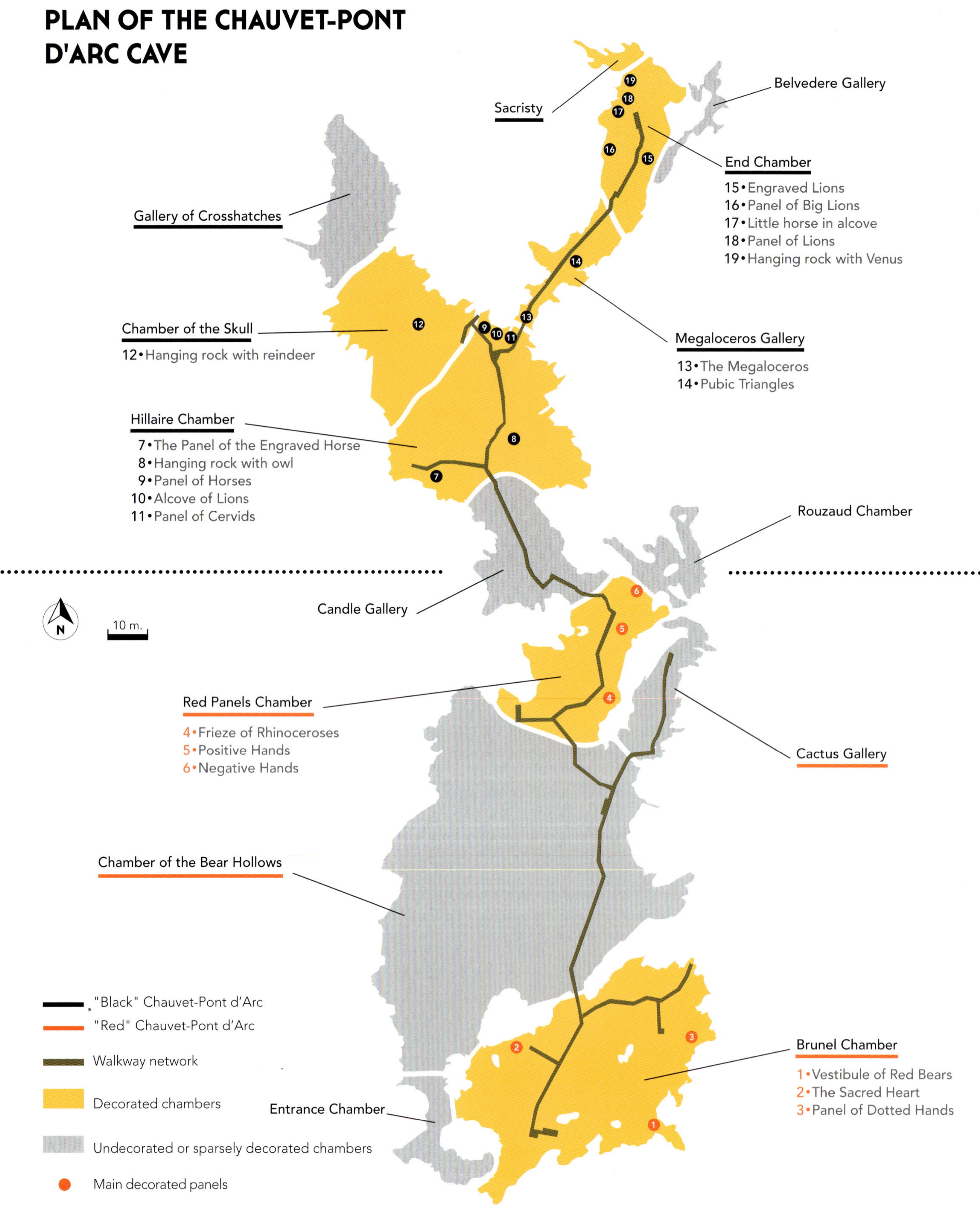

SUMMARY

(pages 6-7)
The Ardèche River carved vertiginous gorges in the limestone massifs over thousands of years.

(following pages)
The Chauvet-Pont d'Arc cave opens out on the Cirque d'Estre cliff facing south, offering an ideal shelter for prehistoric humans.

FORWARD

Transmitting and Sharing the Earliest Art

A visit to the Chauvet-Pont d'Arc cave in the gorges of the Ardèche is a unique, unsettling experience that I had the privilege to share with the discoverers. The walkways now protecting the floor were not yet installed and my steps led me over the miraculously preserved floors of the cavern. For me this was an initiatory path, in a place where man met animal, and left paintings marking the starting point of the history of art some 36,000 years ago. The cavern illustrates the passage of darkness to light, and for the first time in history, this path was taken in the opposite direction: men penetrating the depths of the earth to inscribe their myths in the form of paintings and drawings, revealed by 3D technology in the present work.

How then may we protect and transmit these first accomplished cultural traces of humanity, situated at the beginnings of the history of art? We chose an ambitious replica, in the shape of an integrally reconstituted cavern, with its main mineralogical, paleontological, archaeological and artistic riches. When visiting the Pont-d'Arc Cavern, which reproduces half of the 8,500 square metres of the original cavity, visitors from all over the world will be able to experience the same incomparable emotion as that experienced before the masterpieces of our Aurignacian ancestors.

This was the ambition — and the success — of the numerous scientists, architects, scenographers, surveyors, artists, specialised companies and communities who combined their skills and knowledge to offer the most beautiful reproduction imaginable. Welcome to all those who visit it, all those people coming from the world over to discover the earliest art.

Beyond this, with the opening of the Pont-d'Arc Cavern, the department of the Ardèche takes its place as a new cultural and heritage destination, lent force by the listing of the Chauvet-Pont d'Arc cave as a UNESCO World Heritage Site. By revealing the invisible at the heart of the gorges of the Ardèche River, we offer humanity a veritable initiatory path, guiding present and future generations to our roots as free human beings and universal thinkers.

Pascal Terrasse
President of the *Caverne du Pont-d'Arc Syndicat mixte*,
Secretary General of *the Assemblée parlementaire de la Francophonie.*

PREFACE

The Decorated Cave of Pont d'Arc, better known under the name of *The Chauvet Cave* bears witness to Humanity's very great age: 36,000 years! Beyond its natural wonders, its exceptional cave paintings and astonishing spatial arrangements make it a *"planetary treasure"*. From the majestic Pont d'Arc Bridge overlooking the meander where the cave is situated, the opening of the great overhang that collapsed 22,000 years ago could be seen on the cliff. Miraculously locked away since then, the cavity has reached us in a state of stupefying freshness.

In 1994, its three *"inventors"* (the term used in France for a discoverer), the speleologists, Éliette Brunel, Jean-Marie Chauvet and Christian Hillaire, became the first curators in view of the precautions they took when they discovered it. Guided by the enlightened expertise of the eminent prehistorian Jean Clottes, and convinced of its exceptional universal value, the French state engaged and determined measures for optimum conservation: on January 13th 1995, learning from the experience of Altamira (Spain) and Lascaux (France), two caves exposed to damage from too numerous visitors, the state decided not to open Chauvet to the public. On October 13th 1995, it was put on the list of historical monuments, giving it the greatest degree of legal protection in this way. The state acquired it, protected it from intrusions and created a dedicated conservation service in 2000 to watch over its fragile internal equilibrium, using the most advanced technologies.

The Cave's secrets are "our" secrets, those of "our" Humanity from the earliest times. They could not remain hidden! They had to be brought to the light of day. Conscious of its duty, since 1998 the French state has financed a multidisciplinary team to explore and observe its untouched treasures, forbidding any excavations, authorising only certain studies. The floors with their wealth of archaeological vestiges and the walls with their incredible paintings created by our Aurignacian ancestors can all thus be kept intact. Between 2001 and 2005, the French state invested in the installation of reversible walkways made from inert high-technology alloys making it possible to move inside the cavity: an innovation in the fragile world of decorated caves.

The results obtained by the team of researchers are incredibly rich and diverse. Today we have greater knowledge about the geo-morphological formation of the cavity and its magnificent concretions, and the lives of cave bears and cave lions and woolly rhinoceroses. Above all we discover the life of the human beings of that time through the study of the talented Aurignacians' paintings whose meaning and purpose still remain to be discovered.

How may we transmit these pictures and this knowledge? Modern virtual communication tools allow us to promote the Cave on a worldwide scale. The present work's multimedia enhancement, accessible from every corner of the globe, attests to this, as do the images available on the Internet sites of the French Ministry of Culture or the Pont d'Arc Cavern. The idea of reproducing the Cave near the actual site, contemplated very soon after discovery, became reality on the Razal plateau at Vallon-Pont-d'Arc, under the supervision of the architects *Fabre/ Speller and Atelier 3A*, and under the attentive authority of the joint association responsible for the project. It was financed by a partnership between the French State, regional and local authorities, the European Union and a private company. The replica is called *Pont-d'Arc Cavern – Ardèche*. The revolutionary technologies employed have ensured a reproduction as close as possible to the original Cave thanks to the best professionals from every field: the "hyper-modern" in the service of the "hyper-ancient". And lastly, a scientific committee has guaranteed a faithful reproduction that will profoundly touch the heart and soul of every visitor. The present work contributes to enhancing the planetary importance of the site, which naturally justifies its place on the Heritage of Humanity List.

Aurélie Filippetti
Minister of Culture and Communication
France

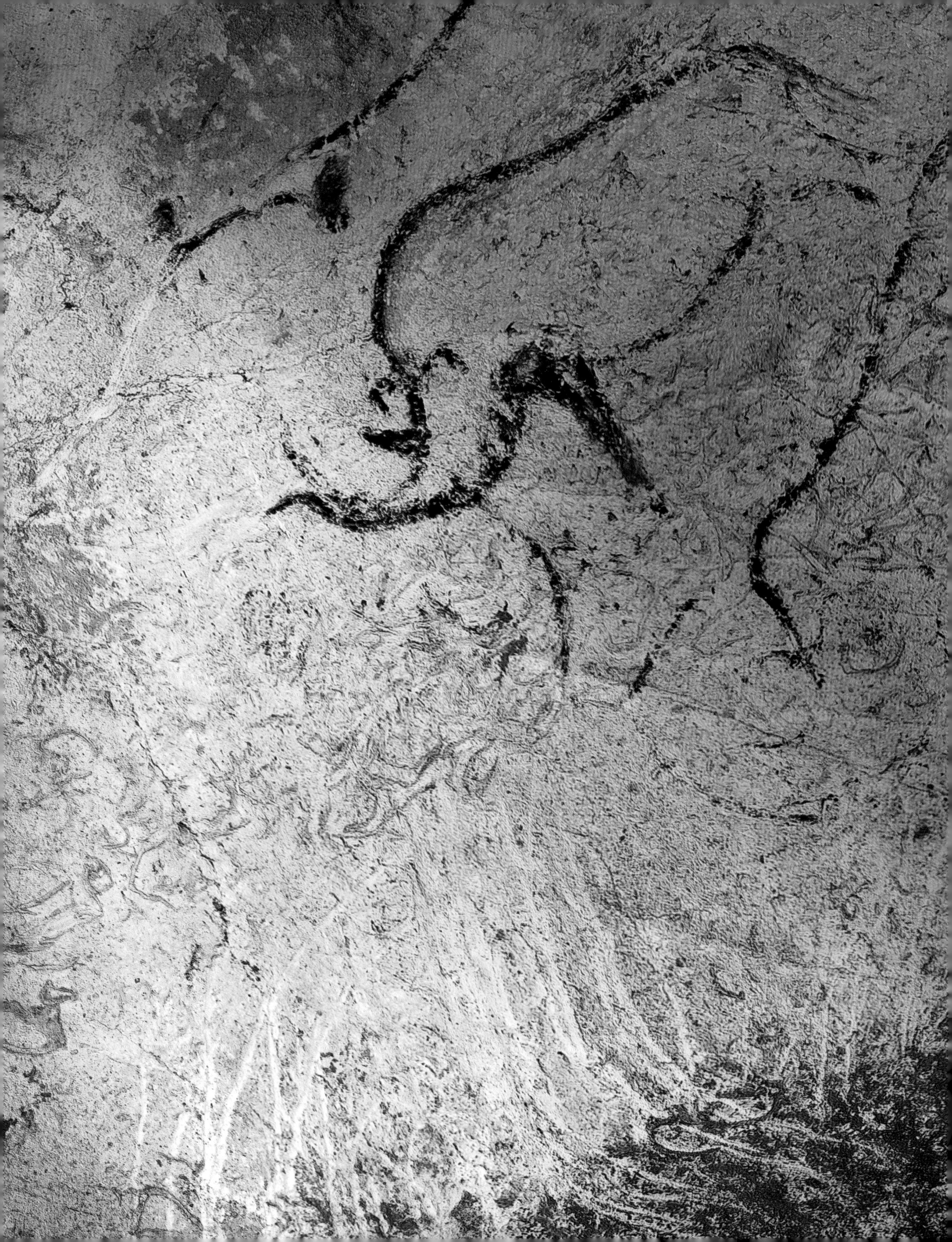

An Experience in Time and Space

The meeting place on that cool morning in May 2014 was at the foot of the majestic cliffs of the Cirque d'Estre, below which reposes the Chauvet-Pont d'Arc cave and its 36,000-year-old paintings and drawings: the oldest works known to this day and the first images of humanity.

To reach this unique site, made still more spectacular by the natural arch of the Pont d'Arc, the best way is through the gorges of the Ardèche River, the same route the Aurignacians must have taken before us. Viewed from the windswept plateau above, the vertical walls plunging towards the river cause vertigo and inspire respect. Like a foretaste of the shock to come… Then, climbing the natural ledge carved in the cliff by cycles of freezing and thawing, one can only approve of our ancestors' choice. The cold, stinging wind gives way to gentle warmth, due to the protection afforded by the wall facing south, which they too must have appreciated. As one moves higher among the green oaks and junipers, it is the whole of the dried-up meander of the Ardèche River that lies at our feet. For them, the view was panoramic and they were able to safely observe the great mammals — aurochs, rhinoceroses and big cats — whose images they later inscribed inside the sanctuary.

Soon we found ourselves in front of the mouth of the cave. Our guides reminded us of the safety measures, one of them typed in the door code on the keypad set into the wall, and a heavy metal door opened and closed behind us. We were inside the first airlock, and soon attired in sterile jumpsuits and helmets. The descent into the depths of the earth is by means of a metal ladder that leads to the first walkway.

The Chauvet-Pont d'Arc cave was there in front of our eyes, in the light of the torches and headlamps. The first, almost oppressive feeling, is the immensity of the space and the enormity of the volumes. The chambers extend as far as the eyes can see, in every direction, and the ceilings are extremely high. Then as we progressed, it was the geological beauty of the cavern that replaced this first impression. The concretions glitter, the curtains sparkle, the chromatic variations in the rock reflect each other from wall to wall, like scales carefully practised over millions of years.

On the ground, another spectacle unfolded, one that was just as poignant. Skeletal remains of bears, mostly skulls, as if petrified by time, could be counted by the hundreds. Here remains of an ibex, there two cave bears' tracks stretching over dozens of yards, the longest path of its kind ever discovered. Still farther on, the first trace of prehistoric man appears, in the shape of a bear humerus deliberately stuck in the loamy earth. What could be the magical reason for this, and in the context of which belief? Unless it was a marker, indicating the symbolic entry of the sanctuary? This remains a mystery.

But we must move on for the visit is limited to two hours to avoid damage to the cave. Suddenly the first decorated panel appears, awaiting us in the darkness. Lights. Here on the wall, dozens of handprints in red ochre. The man of Chauvet-Pont d'Arc is there before us, even more alive because of the seeming freshness of the paint. This underground journey has taken us back 36,000 years to the very origins of art and of symbols: an unprecedented emotion.

INTRODUCTION

As we move through the walkways and past the walls, our enchantment grows. Here is the Panel of Red Rhinoceroses, the Panel of the White Horse traced in clay, then the awe-inspiring composition of Horses, Rhinoceroses, Felines and Reindeer traced in charcoal, stirring in their precision, the mastery of their strokes, their sheer emotional power. This is only to be matched by the unforgettable scene in the last meanders of the cave in which dozens of big cats attack their prey, compelling in their vitality and trueness to life. Beside them, as if in the background of the scene, a stupefying primitive Venus observes us, in the form of two female legs and a pubic triangle executed with a masterful hand on a rock pendant. The eternal, mysterious message of Chauvet-Pont d'Arc, marked as it is by profound humanity, haunts us long after we regretfully leave this first sanctuary held sacred by *Homo sapiens*.

A veritable voyage in time, the exploration of the Chauvet-Pont d'Arc cave is also a powerful sensory experience, which appeals to our deepest perception. In the almost infinitely tortured volumes of the cavern, the body unconsciously searches for visual clues to orientate and direct itself towards the depths of the earth. Let us imagine for a moment the Aurignacians' progression in trembling torchlight in this vast, rugged subterranean world. Once they had discovered the cavity, how many times did they need to visit it? How many patient explorations did they need to imagine and appropriate the three dimensions of its expanse? Our only certitude is that their visualisation of the interior cartography and their composition of a mental image of the cavity were perfect, as witnessed by the structured repartition of the works in the various chambers and on the walls, as well as the masterful use of the contours of the rock to inscribe the animal figures they chose to represent. The art of Chauvet-Pont d'Arc seems to have been prepared and conceived in three dimensions, and only then did the hand of the painter, the engraver and the draughtsman follow in the execution of this ambitious pictorial project—and with what panache!

Is there a better technique then 3D for transmitting, in all its dimensions, this first masterpiece of our shared humanity? What greater homage can we pay to the absolute talent of the Aurignacian masters, the first representatives of a long line of creators that still continues today in every type of contemporary art?

It is the ambition of this work and its digital extension, dedicated to the history of the Chauvet-Pont d'Arc cave, to retrace the major stages from its discovery to its reproduction, as well as its definitive closure to the public and its scientific study. But above all, through the images extracted from the 3D model of the original cavity, to share and transmit the inestimable artistic treasures that remain hidden from view under the cliff of the Cirque d'Estre.

Pedro Lima

(preceding pages)
Engravings and drawings of felines, rhinoceroses and a vulva on the right wall of the End Chamber at Chauvet-Pont d'Arc.

01

THE PONT D'ARC THROUGH THE AGES

A NATURAL MONUMENT CHOSEN BY MAN

Forged by the combined action of water and stone over the ages, the Pont d'Arc, a bridge spanning the Ardèche River, like the cliffs and gorges that line its tumultuous waters, constitutes an exceptional natural site. A monumental backdrop that could only have impressed prehistoric humans and guided them to their most beautiful sanctuary.

◆

Where did the artists of the Chauvet-Pont d'Arc cave come from more than 40,000 years ago, those men who belonged to tribes that occupied the Ardèche region of today? And more precisely the majestic setting of the Pont d'Arc, the bridge that spans the capricious river near the Cirque d'Estre, marking the entrance to its long, deep, winding gorges? Did these groups living in the prehistoric time known as the Aurignacian period travel upstream from the valley of the Rhône river, thirty kilometres from there, following its numerous detours? Or did they descend from the plateaus beyond the steep cliffs overlooking the Ardèche valley? Whatever the case, no doubt these newcomers stood spellbound before the extraordinary beauty of this site, just as visitors do today. The 60 metre-wide limestone arch of the Pont d'Arc appears to have been cast above the waters by a giant hand. Higher than 30 metres, it seems to remain suspended in space, creating an impression of power and majesty. This impression is further strengthened by the equally spectacular, grandiose landscape surrounding it. On the left bank of the Ardèche River, an ancient broad meander is hemmed in by a cliff in a rounded shape more than 180 metres high. The geological history of the Cirque d'Estre, the present-day name of this limestone formation in the shape of a loop, is inseparably linked to that of the Pont d'Arc. During its long course beginning in the Vivarais region, 100 kilometres from here, the Ardèche patiently carved its way through the limestone massifs of the region. But a rocky ledge blocked its path a little beyond the present-day village of Vallon-Pont d'Arc. To avoid this natural barrier, the river first dug a meander, the actual Cirque d'Estre, exposing the imposing cliffs surrounding it over the ages. But circa 400,000 years ago, the uninterrupted action of the water on the rocky barrier, on its surface and in depth, ended by breaching the natural dam. Consequently, the Cirque d'Estre meander slowly dried up and the impetuous river continued its incessant work downstream, eroding the limestone massif and giving the gorges their present vertiginously abrupt profile.

The Pont d'Arc Bridge, which peaks thirty metres above the river, is the result of water erosion on a rock barrier opening a breach circa 400,000 years ago.

Even more striking, the shape of the Pont d'Arc viewed from downstream suggests a mammoth with a round belly facing left, a bump protruding from its head, the arched line of its back, with two legs—fore and hind—that seem to plunge into the river. Is it possible that the Aurignacians who discovered this site almost 40,000 years ago saw in the stone monument, emerging at that time from a sparse forest of fir trees, the emblematic image of a mighty mammoth, hunted, feared and respected all at once? It is entirely possible since Palaeolithic societies of hunter-gatherers living in complete osmosis with nature must have been sensitive to all the mineral and plant forms surrounding them.

Already greatly impressed by the spectacle of the stone bridge that allowed them to cross the river, the Aurignacians must also have been attracted by another particularity of the landscape, accentuating still further its visual impact. Above the dried-up meander, several dozen yards from the Pont d'Arc, an immense overhang opened up on the side of the cliff, ten metres high and twelve metres wide, visible from a great distance.

(Discovery)

Overview of the Cirque d'Estre and visit of the Chauvet-Pont d'Arc cave from the entrance to the Skull Chamber.

The natural shape of the Pont d'Arc Bridge (above) resembles a mammoth, and the Chauvet-Pont d'Arc artists may have remarked this. Opposite: view of the cut-off meander of the Ardèche River. The topography of the landscape has hardly changed since the Upper Palaeolithic period.

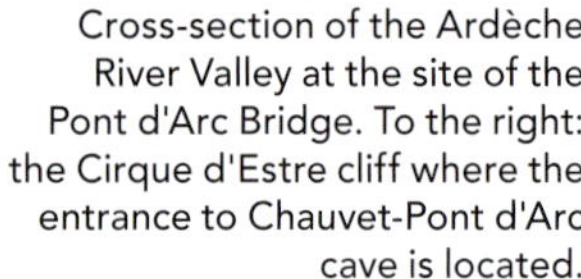

Cross-section of the Ardèche River Valley at the site of the Pont d'Arc Bridge. To the right: the Cirque d'Estre cliff where the entrance to Chauvet-Pont d'Arc cave is located.

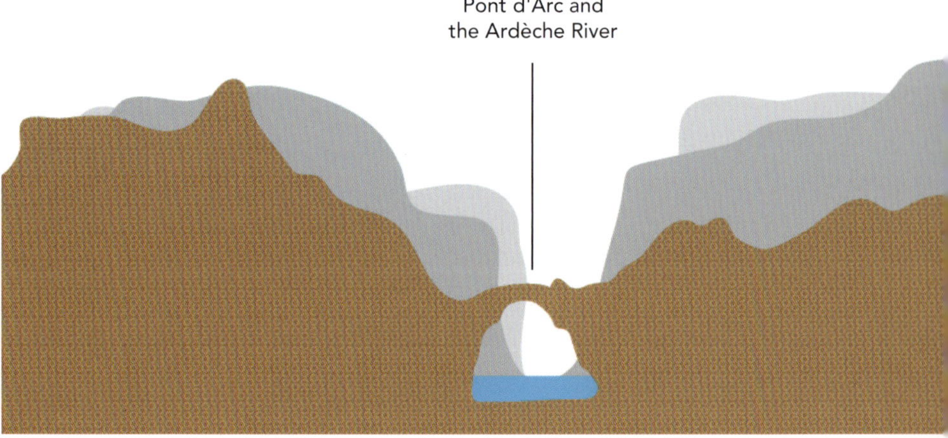

View today of the dried-up meander of the Ardèche River. The entrance to the Chauvet-Pont d'Arc cave, which has since collapsed, was located here 36,000 years ago.

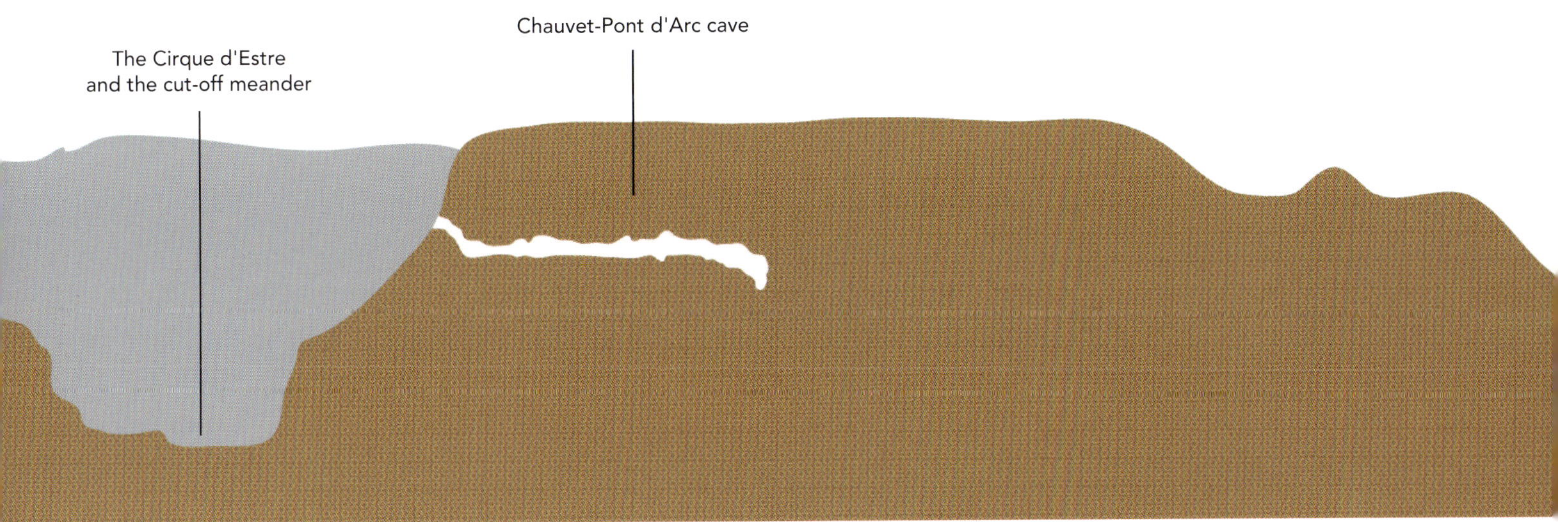

For the prehistorian Jean-Michel Geneste, director of the scientific team of the Chauvet-Pont d'Arc cave, the association of the Pont d'Arc bridge and the vast opening in the cliff may have constituted a sort of system of geographic markers, a dual topographical landmark, rendering this unique landscape sacred for humans. To such a degree that it led them to this cavity on the rock wall in order to occupy it and choose to transform it into a sanctuary dedicated to their myths and beliefs by creating hundreds of paintings, engravings and drawings there.

Today, this gaping hole in the cliff has completely disappeared from the landscape. About 22,000 years ago, the weight of the rock above the overhang caused it to collapse and completely obscure the cavity. This event also ensured that the cave and the treasures it contains were perfectly preserved. And so it came to pass that in 1994, the speleologist Jean-Marie Chauvet and his two colleagues, Éliette Brunel and Christian Hillaire, rediscovered the Pont d'Arc cave by crawling through a narrow passage above the original entrance. A cave occupied nearly 40,000 years ago by their distant predecessors, and forgotten ever since.

A Cavity Visible From a Great Distance

(above)
Panorama of the Cirque d'Estre cliff today, with the entrance to the Chauvet-Pont d'Arc cave. To the right: the overhang 36,000 years ago, with an opening ten metres high and twelve wide. (Source: B. Sadier / Edytem).

(opposite)
Prehistoric humans reached the cavity by this natural ledge, carved in the side of the cliff by erosion. It is still used by hikers and scientists.

A Culture Structured on a Continental Scale

Who were these Aurignacians of the Ardèche, creators of the sumptuous Chauvet-Pont d'Arc cave? Like all representatives of the four main cultures that succeeded each other during the Upper Palaeolithic (Aurignacian, Gravettian, Solutrean, Magdalenian) between -42,000 and -12,000 years, they lived grouped in nomadic tribes that followed the seasonal migrations of the wild animals they hunted over vast distances. The Aurignacian artisans fashioned refined, sharp tools, and easy-to-handle light blades and knives out of stone, bone, reindeer antler and ivory, which allowed them to cut and prepare the meat of the large herbivores, mainly reindeer, that they captured. Another characteristic of Aurignacian tools: their progressive miniaturisation over time, culminating in tiny blades around 32,000 years ago. These tools, called microliths, were easily carried over long distances, and were therefore perfectly adapted to the itinerant lifestyle of the Aurignacians. Their homogenous culture stretched over the whole of the European continent, from the Atlantic Ocean to Central Europe, and possibly even farther. Anatomically, the Aurignacian resembles us since he belongs to the same species, *Homo sapiens*. He possessed the same intellectual capacities and was tall, more that 1.8 metres in height on average.

-2.9 million years

LOWER PALAEOLITHIC

First tools fashioned in stone
Discovery of fire

-300,000 years

MIDDLE PALAEOLITHIC

Elaborate tools fashioned in stone
Appearance of symbolism
(ornaments, use of ochre)

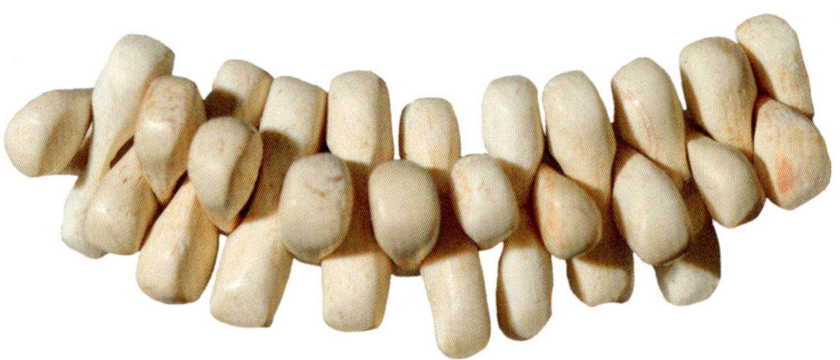

Palaeolithic artisans fashioned sharp stone tools like the Aurignacian blade above, found at the La Ferrassie site, and ornaments like this bracelet made from seashells. *Collections of the Musée national de préhistoire, Les Eyzies-de-Tayac, France.*

Vulvas were engraved on this rock dating from the Aurignacian period, discovered at the La Ferrassie site in Dordogne (France). This theme is found on the walls of the Chauvet-Pont d'Arc cave. *Collections of the Musée national de préhistoire at Eyzies-de-Tayac, France.*

MAJOR PREHISTORIC AND UPPER PALAEOLITHIC PERIODS

-42,000 years

-12,000 years

UPPER PALAEOLITHIC

AURIGNACIAN → GRAVETTIAN → SOLUTREAN → MAGDALENIAN

AURIGNACIAN
-42,000 to -34,000
Bone-pointed spears, stone bladelets and knives
Half-animal, half-human statuettes
Chauvet-Pont d'Arc Cave (Ardèche)

GRAVETTIAN
-34,000 to -26,500
Female statuettes called Venuses
Cussac Cave (Dordogne)

SOLUTREAN
-26,500 to -22,000
Sophisticated fashioning of flint
Invention of spear-thrower and eyed needle
Caves of Lascaux (Dordogne) and Cosquer (Bouches-du-Rhône)

MAGDALENIAN
-22,000 to -12,000
Caves of Altamira (Cantabria, Spain), Lascaux (Dordogne) and Niaux (Ariège)

When they arrived in the Ardèche circa 40,000 years ago, the Aurignacians were not the first representatives of the genus *Homo* to set foot in the region. Humans were already present there 300,000 years ago, on the site of Orgnac. Neanderthal Man prospered circa 100,000 years ago, as witnessed by some fifteen archaeological sites where tools were found. Like the Gravettian, Solutrean and Magdalenian peoples who succeeded them, the Aurignacian tribes of Ardèche inhabited sporadic hunting spots, camping in rock shelters at the foot of cliffs, on the trails of reindeer, horses, aurochs or bison, which were their principal food source. They also found shelter at the entrances of the more spacious, sunny cavities situated close to the river. These gorges offered a microclimate providing strong sunlight and protection from the winds due to the presence of rocky cirques and rugged cliffs. This was a welcome respite since during the coldest period of the ice age, circa -18,000 years, temperatures could drop to -20°C in winter, and the plateaus were windswept. In the era of the Chauvet-Pont d'Arc cave, the annual mean temperature was 4.5°C lower than at the present time, corresponding to temperatures in the south of Norway today. On the plateaus, the landscape resembled a grassy steppe, with freezing winds. As for the valleys, they contained trees, disseminated in forests that were not as dense and thick as they are today. The trees were mostly birch, juniper and fir, as shown by the pollens found on archaeological sites and confirmed by laboratory analysis.

Human presence in the Ardèche is recorded 300,000 years ago, and the Neanderthal man thrived here about 100,000 years ago.

The Ardèche constituted an important artistic region during the Upper Palaeolithic period, counting some twenty decorated sites.

PREHISTORIC SITES AND DECORATED CAVES OF THE ARDÈCHE, WITH DISCOVERY DATES

Chabot cave
Engravings
1878

Oulen cave
Paintings and Engravings
1907, 1951

Ranc-Pointu cave
Engravings
1908

Ebbou cave
Engravings
1946

Colombier cave
Engravings
1976

Deux Ouvertures cave
Engravings
1985

Tête du Lion cave
Paintings
1993

Chauvet-Pont d'Arc cave
Engravings and Paintings
1994

(Left to right)
Scraper on blade, scale nucleus and scraper on flake blade discovered around fireplaces at the Ardèche shelter of Les Pêcheurs, dated to the Aurignacian period. *Collections of the Musée régional de préhistoire, Aven d'Orgnac, France*

(Knowledge)

Palaeolithic parietal art between -36,000 years and -12,000 years.

•

During their long marches in the gorges of the Ardèche during the glacial age, or while lying in wait for their prey behind high grasses, the Aurignacian hunters observed the animals surrounding them at length. These were the very animals later represented in the caves devoted to their spiritual practices, which they decorated with numerous figures. There is the horse, often hunted and represented, the two-horned woolly rhinoceros, protected by a thick coat of fur, the aurochs and the bison that lived in small herds, and the musk ox, that still lives in the polar regions today. And finally the reindeer, under-represented on the walls of decorated caves, but which constituted the mainstay of the diet of Upper Palaeolithic humans. As for the ibex, at home on steep, rocky terrains, it was omnipresent in the gorges of the Ardèche.

The same was true of the cave bear that hibernated in the open caverns on the sides of cliffs, and which must have impressed humans by its strength and size: more than three metres tall when standing on its hind legs! The Aurignacians were most certainly also impressed by the agility and cruelty of the felines that roamed the surrounding plateaus and valleys, pitilessly springing on the herds of aurochs. These large cats may only have cowered in front of the terrible curved horns of the charging woolly rhinoceroses, which also form a part of this rich Palaeolithic lexicon of animals, conducive to peopling myths and beliefs. The tribes watched the elaborate and complex behaviour (stalking, hunting, courtship, mating, combats) of these many species for hours on end while patiently lying in wait in protected observation posts. Later, plunged in darkness, they transcribed these images of life and death on the walls of the cave-sanctuaries.

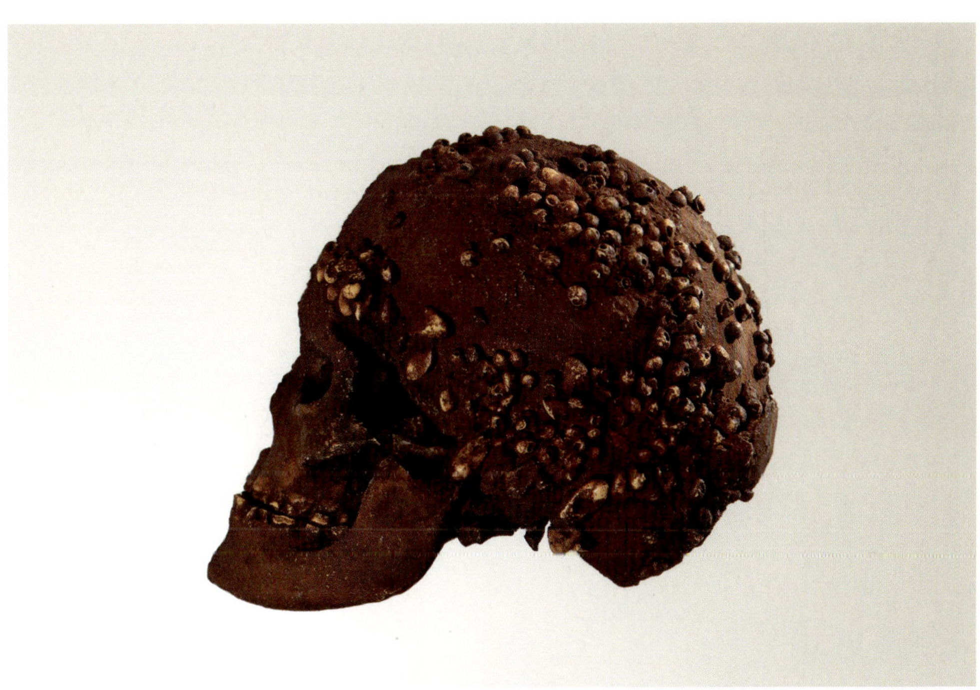

Skull from the "Lady of Cavillon" grave (Grimaldi caves, Italy), dating to the Upper Palaeolithic, decorated with more than two hundred seashells and painted in red ochre and black hematite.

Refinement and an Elaborate Spiritual Life

Like all *Homo sapiens*, the Aurignacians enjoyed a rich and elaborate spiritual life. They expressed it through the burial of the dead, like that of several children whose graves were unearthed along the riverside. Their ornaments, made with beads of soft rock, pierced animal teeth or shells exchanged over hundreds of kilometres demonstrate their refinement. The complexity of their spiritual vision is evident above all in the form of engravings, drawings and paintings—essentially of animals—in caves made sacred by such symbols. This artistic and religious practice is called parietal or cave art, and it continued during the whole of the Upper Palaeolithic, from -37,000 to -12,000 years, in the Ardèche region and throughout the entire continent of Europe. In this way, even before the discovery of the Chauvet-Pont d'Arc cave and its fabulous artistic treasures, the Ardèche, along with some twenty other decorated sites, already represented a major artistic region. And this is the case even if it remained in the background compared with the great cultural centres of the Franco-Cantabria area on both sides of the Pyrenees Mountains, or the Dordogne. It is even in the Ardèche that the first known decorated cavern was discovered in 1878, the Chabot cave of mammoths... one year before Altamira, in Spain. At Baume d'Oulen, midway between the river and the plateau, *Homo sapiens* represented mammoths in red ochre and mysterious signs in the shape of brackets crossed with dots. Other consecrated sanctuaries between the Aurignacian and Magdalenian periods include the Ebbou cave, with among others, its very stylised small engraved horse, the Colombier rock shelter containing a large ibex with a finely engraved head and duplicate legs as though the artist meant to represent movement. Or the Deux Ouvertures cave, a hidden Aurignacian sanctuary with its opening on the promontory called "Ranc-Pointu", almost at the end of the gorges of the Ardèche. It includes a bison's body filled with crosshatches, a provocative "Venus" with stylised feminine contours, and a sleek feline. All these sites were already indispensable for understanding our origins, particularly concerning the spiritual and the artistic. Then in the winter of 1994 came the discovery that upset everything.

(above)
The "Venus of Willendorf", a statuette sculpted in limestone dating to the Gravettian period, was discovered in Lower Austria in 1908. It was probably originally painted in red ochre.

(opposite)
"Lion Man", an Aurignacian statuette discovered in the Stadel cave in the Swabian Jura (Germany) in 1939, is reminiscent of certain anthropomorphised lion figures in the End Chamber of the Chauvet-Pont d'Arc cave.

02

FROM DISCOVERY TO SCIENTIFIC STUDY

The unsettling revelation of the origins of art

In January 1995, the world learned of the major discovery of a cave decorated with hundreds of magnificent drawings in the south of France. It was the beginning of the extraordinary scientific and artistic adventure of the Chauvet-Pont d'Arc cave, which continues today.

◆

The starting point of this incredible discovery began a few weeks earlier, on Sunday, December 18th 1994, around 3 p.m. On this cool, sunny winter afternoon, Éliette Brunel, Christian Hillaire and Jean-Marie Chauvet, three experienced speleologists who were also friends, visited the grandiose landscape of the Cirque d'Estre, a circular cliff that marks the entrance to the gorges of the Ardèche River. Their objective: to explore the subterranean wealth of their region as they had already done for many years. They used a well-tried method for this: testing the walls by passing their hands or their faces along the fissures, in search of the slightest whisper of air. For if they felt a breath of air, it certainly meant that there was a shaft, an abyss or a cavity there, just behind the rock.

On that particular afternoon, it was precisely such a puff of air, observed a few weeks earlier at the bottom of a crevice on the side of a cliff that the three explorers intended to inspect. To reach it, they took the old bridle path leading through green oaks and boxwood. When they arrived at the foot of the small cavity, the speleologists entered it in single file, and a little farther on they stumbled upon rocks, which they extracted one by one. The breath of air was still there, still persistent. Then they came upon a narrow clayey passage where they had to crawl on all fours. Still several metres farther on, they came upon an open hole in the roof of a vast cavity. The floor was visible ten metres below in the halo of their miner's headlamps. Their excitement was at its peak, and the group decided to return to the truck to fetch a ladder. The night was black and starry on the Cirque d'Estre when the three speleologists once again went underground, descending into a vast cavity, until that day unknown to the world.

At first glance, even in feeble light, the discovery seemed a major one: immense vaults, majestic volumes, monumental limestone columns, sparkling limestone draperies and veils. The cave was endowed with extraordinary mineral beauty, as though inviolate for thousands of years. Were they the first to penetrate this underground sanctuary? Still astounded by what they had just seen, the three explorers decided to enter a second chamber, even larger than the first. There they made out fossilized skeletal remains, bear skulls and teeth by the dozens, all intact, on a perfectly preserved loamy floor, which incited them to step carefully in order not to damage these precious vestiges.

(opposite)
A positive handprint obtained by covering the hand in red ochre and placing it on the wall: here, in the Red Panels Chamber at Chauvet-Pont d'Arc.

(following pages)
The imposing volumes of the Chamber of the Bear Hollows: this was the first chamber the Aurignaciens reached from the original entrance.

"They Were Here!"

But the major shock was still to come in another gallery, even narrower than the preceding one. All of a sudden, Éliette Brunel distinguished two lines painted in red ochre on the wall, and cried out: *"They were here!"* Yes, humans had been here, undoubtedly thousands of years ago, to paint and draw. Over many hours the discoveries came in succession, each more incredible than the next: here a small red mammoth on a rocky spur and a massive bear. Farther on, an insect and a butterfly, an owl, and there a horse and a mammoth both engraved on the soft limestone wall covered in clay. Then in another large chamber, the first masterpiece appeared, and took their breath away: dozens of horses, aurochs, felines, reindeer and black rhinoceroses overlapped on the length of a vast wall that had been scraped beforehand, and was later named the Panel of Horses, a consummately executed work in black charcoal by a prehistoric Michelangelo. Overwhelmed by what they had seen, the three discoverers left the site, careful not to disturb the floors as they did so.

A Masterpiece for Eternity

They returned a week later, on Christmas eve, protecting the floors this time with a long band of plastic sheeting, and accompanied by three colleagues, Daniel André, Michel Chabaud and Jean-Louis Payan. Once at the bottom of the cavity, a still unexplored last chamber contained a sublime revelation, which was to definitively propel the cave into history. There, unfolding on twelve metres of golden wall, a fresco unique in all of prehistoric art: pictorial fireworks that associated felines by

(above)
Numerous depressions dot the floors of the Chamber of the Bear Hollows (visible in the foreground), made by the bodies of the cave bears during their long hibernation.

(opposite)
The three discovers of the Chauvet-Pont d'Arc cave: Christian Hillaire, Éliette Brunel and Jean-Marie Chauvet (left to right) pose close to the cavity's present entrance.

the dozen, powerful rhinoceros represented in perspective, a herd of bison and a small horse as if huddled in an alcove. Farther on, a rocky spur was decorated with an overwhelming mi-human, mi-bison motif: a founding myth coming straight from the depths of time. *"We all had tears in our eyes, and we constantly wondered if we were in a waking dream,"* one of the discoverers later recounted. Yes, the cavity concealed under the cliffs of the Cirque d'Estre was a major masterpiece of cave art, and of the art of humanity, equal to Lascaux in the Dordogne, Cosquer in Provence or Altamira in Spanish Cantabria. The time had now come to share this masterpiece with the world.

Alerted on December 28th 1994, the prehistorian Jean Clottes, specialist in Palaeolithic cave art, came to the site to authenticate the discovery. He went underground in the company of the three discoverers, Jean-Pierre Daugas, Regional Curator for Archaeology for the Rhône-Alpes region, and his deputy Bernard Gély. The prehistorian was sceptical: the inventors invoked, amongst others, the dozens of rhinoceroses, whereas barely twenty are referenced in all of prehistoric Europe. In spite of his reservations, once he arrived in front of the decorated walls, Jean Clottes was dazzled: the cave was a marvel, both geologically and artistically. Before the stupendous Panel of Horses, brought to light ten days earlier by Chauvet and his friends, and then contemplating the incredible Feline Profiles in the End Chamber the prehistorian felt, by his own testimony, one of the greatest emotions in his career as a researcher, and in his entire life. He spent six long hours in the magical cave with the rest of the group going from one discovery to the next. At first glance, he was certain of the authenticity of the drawings, which later dating techniques and studies were to confirm. This authenticity was further corroborated by the presence of micro-crystallizations inside the site's numerous engravings, resulting from several thousand years of the geological activity of the walls. Other clues such as the virgin floors and a great number of intact fossilized bear skulls provided further confirmation, dispelling any possibility of a fake.

(above)
The prehistorian Jean Clottes authenticated the Chauvet-Pont d'Arc drawings and paintings on December 28th 1994, and led the scientific team's study from 1998 to 2002.

(opposite)
The Brunel Chamber is mostly decorated with paintings and red dots. The panel above right suggests the shape of a rhinoceros.

(below)
We find cave bears' skeletal remains throughout the Chauvet-Pont d'Arc cave, as seen here in the Hillaire Chamber. Questions remain concerning the chronology of the cohabitations of men and bears in the cavity.

Three weeks later, on January 18th 1995, the Ministry of Culture organized a press conference in Paris. On that occasion the minister Jacques Toubon, along with the three discoverers, revealed the existence of the Chauvet cave and its fabulous treasures. Unsurprisingly, the impact was immediate in France and abroad, and widely reported by the media. The cave now belonged to all of humanity.

◆

From the very first months following discovery and later in the course of research, more than 80 charcoal samples were taken for dating purposes from a number of drawings, as well as traces on the walls that resulted from the artists blowing on torches to revive the flame for lighting their work, or from the hearths on the floor of the cavity. All these analyses make Chauvet-Pont d'Arc the best dated decorated cave in the world today. Announced in the month of June 1995, the first results obtained by the carbon 14 method fell like a bombshell. With dates placed around 31,000 years before the present (BP), the drawings in the Ardèche cavity are therefore the oldest known to us. Since then, and after carbon 14 calibration, two groups of dates were obtained: circa 35,500 ±1000 for the oldest, corresponding to the execution of the drawings; and between 30,000 and 31,000 for the second group, corresponding to the passage of men who probably did not leave any artistic traces. With an age of 36,000 years, the magnificent drawings of the Chauvet-Pont d'Arc cave are thus both the most technically masterful, for their command of tone and perspective, and humanity's oldest. To give an example, the works of Chauvet-Pont d'Arc date from the Aurignacian period, the first real Upper Palaeolithic culture in Europe, making them twice as old as the famous Lascaux paintings discovered in 1940 in the cave along the Vézère Valley in the Perigord. Chauvet's discovery in 1995 upset all our previous ideas about the origins and the evolution of art, as well as those about our ancestors' intelligence and cognitive capacities. Further discoveries in the cave were to follow.

The geo-morphologist Benjamin Sadier, member of the scientific team, maps the various geological formations in the Cactus Gallery. The white calcite columns and cactus-shaped stalagmites were formed after the Aurignacians' occupation. In the foreground: a pile of rocks assembled by humans.

More than eighty samples of charcoal from the cavity have been dated with ^{14}C, revealing ages between -36,000 and -31,000 years.

Protecting the Cave for Future Generations

As soon as its discovery was announced, in view of its exceptional artistic value, the Chauvet-Pont d'Arc cave symbolically entered the shared heritage of humanity. It was up to the French state to ensure its protection, and to scientists to unlock its secrets. The cavity has reached us in a remarkable state of conservation, due to the closing of its original entrance after the departure of the artists. All those privileged to visit it stress the extraordinary freshness of the pigments, the unspoiled state of the floors and the walls. *"As if each time we enter the front door, the artists leave the cave by the back,"* comments Dominique Baffier, Chauvet's curator between 2000 and 2014.

The cave's protection was put into place after it was acquired from its owners and listed as an historical monument on October 13th 1995. Prior to that, the gendarmerie assured surveillance of the site, and on January 13th, the discoverers had a metal door installed at the entrance to the vestibule at the mouth of the cave, and this was later reinforced. Public access was strictly forbidden and the Ministry of Culture undertook extensive works to safeguard and secure the premises. A heavy armoured door, linked to a 24-hour video-surveillance system closed the vestibule, which was enlarged to facilitate access to researchers and the rare visitors granted admission. The trap-door accessing the vault of the first chamber was enlarged and two fixed ladders made it possible to descend to the ground.

To insure its surveillance and the stability of its environment, two specialized laboratories installed sensors that continuously record several parameters: air, ground and wall temperatures, hygrometry, gaseous exchanges with the outside, levels of carbon dioxide and radon, a radioactive gas that forms naturally in underground environments. By means of these analyses, the best periods for visits and future scientific studies are determined in spring and in autumn. Biologists also take samples to identify possible spores, bacteria or algae that may alter the equilibrium of the cavity or contaminate it. The French state aims at all cost to avoid the same errors committed at Lascaux, an artistic treasure threatened with deterioration due to an excessive number of visits in the years following its discovery. The Ministry of Culture ordered the installation of a network of stainless steel walkways measuring 350 metres long and 60 centimetres wide that follow the path taken by the discoverers. Removable walkways were added to this primary network to facilitate the approach to specific vestiges on the ground or the descent into depressions or collapses, as for example in the Hillaire Chamber.

(above, left to right)
Scientists and visitors enter the cavity by a metallic ladder leading to the Brunel Chamber.

To protect the perfectly preserved floors, the scientists make their studies from the stainless steel walkways, some of which are moveable.

The Panel of the Sacred Heart in the Brunel Chamber is studied from the walkway.

The climatic parameters of the cave are constantly recorded. Here a conservation agent verifies a CO_2 captor.

(Knowledge)

The scientific importance of the Chauvet-Pont d'Arc cave.

(opposite)
Jean-Michel Geneste heads the scientific team at the Chauvet-Pont d'Arc cave. Here he is seen in front of the armoured door protecting the modern entrance.

THE NECESSITY FOR PRESERVATION

In 2000, the French Ministry of Culture and Communication created a service to guarantee the preservation of the Chauvet-Pont d'Arc cave at a high level of excellence. Marie Bardisa succeeded Dominique Baffier as the cavity's curator in 2014. Charles Chauveau, Paulo Rodrigues and Nicolas Lateur assist her in this task. Placed on on-call duty 24/24h, the team works toward the maintenance of optimum conditions to ensure that the cavity is handed down in its present authentic state to future generations.

The cave's climatology is permanently monitored by means of automated readings every fifteen minutes. Air, ground and wall temperatures are measured in three different points in the cavity. The scientific team's paleo-climatologists punctually take additional measurements using water drop counters and temperature captors, as well as samplings of water and calcite.

The level of CO_2 measured in the Chamber of the Bear Hollows and the End Chamber varies from the lowest readings recorded in the Chamber of the Bear Hollows at 1%, to the highest readings recorded in the End Chamber at 4.5%, prohibiting access during many months of the year.

The level of radon on average is 5,500 Bq/m³ with peaks at 15,000 Bq/m³. Labour laws authorise maximum presence in the cavity 60 hours per year and per employee.

As if each time we enter the front door, the artists leave the cave by the back...

Scientists Go into Action

Alongside these extensive works, the Ministry of Culture issued a tender to scientists in the autumn of 1995 with the objective of selecting a team to study the cave and its artworks. The following spring, an international jury chose the team trained and led by Jean Clottes, whose study began in 1998. Since then, the multidisciplinary team composed of some fifty specialists in different areas enters the cave during two annual two-week missions in May and October. The first subject of study is parietal art. Each researcher is in charge of one sector of the cave, where he makes a series of photographs of each panel, which are then printed on paper. Once again in front of the drawings and paintings, the scientist copies all the marks visible on the wall on a transparency placed over the photograph, in order to record every information and every complexity: the superposition of lines, the presence of engravings and bear scratches, finger marks or objects stuck in the rock.

Other specialists concentrate on the traces and the objects on the ground, attesting to the occupation of the cavern by humans and animals (bears, ibexes, canids): prints, hearths and skeletal remains. Another branch of research is called geomorphology, which reconstitutes the geological processes that led to the present shape of the cavity. Finally, the study of pollens introduced by men and animals makes it possible to discover and identify the familiar plants of their milieu.

Thanks to the work of the scientific team, led by Jean-Michel Geneste of the National Prehistory Centre since 2002, we are quite knowledgeable today about the extraordinary art of the Chauvet-Pont d'Arc cave, and its geological and archaeological context. However, research is far from finished given the archaeological wealth of the site, and it benefits constantly from new techniques. Many generations of researchers will follow each other in the fabulous Chauvet-Pont d'Arc cave, which has not yet stopped revealing its secrets.

(below)
Panel of Horses in the Hillaire Chamber: researchers reach it by means of the walkway network.

(opposite)
When investigating the ground near the overhang at the original entrance, the researchers Bernard Gély (left) and Jean-Michel Geneste discovered a stratum of human occupation under the piles of scree that blocked the entrance to the cave 21,500 years ago.

(following pages)
In the Hillaire Chamber, the geo-morphologist Jean-Jacques Delannoy, scientific team member, discovered that the piles of rocks (visible to the left in the foreground) were arranged by man. In the background: Panel of the Engraved Horse.

03

THE CAVE IN ALL ITS DIMENSIONS

The 3D adventure inside Chauvet-Pont d'Arc

In order to understand the cavity's complex volumes, as well as its archaeological and artistic treasures, the necessity of making a 3D copy was recognised in the years following its discovery. With the technical advances made since then, the 3D digital model of the Chauvet-Pont d'Arc cave today constitutes an irreplaceable tool for the conservation, the study, the reproduction, and the dissemination of the earliest works of art.

When they first set foot in the Chauvet-Pont d'Arc cave in December 1994, the three discoverers realized they were awakening, after thousands of years of slumber, a cavity of exceptional dimensions. This was due as much to its length, extending from the mouth of the entrance to the last chamber, as to the vertiginous height of its vaults, and the width of its vast rooms. The grandiose character of this underground jewel was moreover accentuated by its mineralogical wealth and perfection: limestone curtains and domes, stalagmite forests, and delicate, jagged, translucent concretions. Everything here contributes to its magic and enchantment. Such volumes are unknown in the Ardèche gorges, and one must go as far as the Aven Orgnac 15 km southwards to find such a spacious cave.

How then was it possible to render such a complex and immense space? Based on their numerous explorations inside the miraculous cave, always prudently walking on the network of bands of plastic sheeting covering the clayey floor, the three discovers established a preliminary plan of the site during the months following the cave's revelation. In particular, they measured the length of the cave — hollowed out in the course of thousands of years by water infiltrating the limestone plateau — which extends over some 250 metres under the cliff of the Cirque d'Estre. They also gave their definitive names to the major chambers of the cavity: Brunel Chamber, Hillaire Chamber, Chamber of the Bear Hollows, Skull Chamber, End Chamber, Gallery of Crosshatches, Megaloceros Chamber.

In 1997, the French state commissioned the surveyors of the *Cabinet Guy Perazio* to make the first topographical survey of the cavity and its approaches. This recording of data is made with an instrument called a theodolite, which records measurements in three dimensions in space. After 120 days of surveying inside the cavity and some 60,000 measurements, Guy Perazio, assisted by his colleague Guy Bournay and Jean-Marie Chauvet, established the exact measurements of the Chauvet-Pont d'Arc cave that were indispensable both for protecting it and conducting a scientific study. The cave, located 76 metres beneath the plateau, measures exactly 242 metres from its entrance to its deepest recess, a pocket at the bottom of the End Chamber called the Sacristy. Its surface area covers 8,500 square metres, and its total area including walls, floors, and ceilings attains 11,500 square metres. The Chamber of Bear Hollows, so

Laser scanners make it possible to record underground volumes with a resolution approaching one tenth of a millimetre.

called since the cave bears left numerous holes formed by their sleeping bodies during hibernation, is both the widest (50 metres) and the longest (75 metres). As for the highest ceiling, that of the Hillaire Chamber, it reaches 30 metres in height. Farther on, the Gallery of Crosshatches, symmetrical to the End Chamber, only measures 1.5 to 3 metres high, due to a thick loamy deposit on the ground.

In this way the topographical survey made it possible to visualize the cave in three dimensions for the first time. It was also indispensable for installing the vast network of metal walkways allowing the rare visitors and scientists to move within the cave. This network, 350 metres long in total, follows the initial path of the discoverers, preserving in this way most of the perfectly conserved clay soils and the precious vestiges they contain: charred remains of fires used for lighting and making charcoal pigment; traces of an adolescent's footprints; bear, canid and ibex prints; as well as hundreds of skeletal remains and skulls of cave bears. Among these fossilized remains, a bear skull intentionally placed on a rock fallen from the roof has intrigued all the visitors to the cavity since its discovery. Was this act part of a rite or a ceremony? Was there an aesthetic intention? It is impossible to reply to this question on the basis of present research. Whatever the case, the inestimable value of this perfectly preserved vestige alone justifies forbidding everyone from leaving the paths established by the installation of the walkways in 1997. The scientists themselves observe the cavity's decorated walls, archaeological objects or geological structures only from these walkways, using binoculars when necessary.

This concern for protection, which also led the French state to close the cave to the public, springs from the desire to hand it down intact to future generations of researchers in the hope that they will possess techniques capable of revealing information that is still inaccessible today. The problem is that this limits the work of contemporary scientists, particularly in the largest chambers, where the vestiges are sometimes found several metres from the walkways. For instance, in the End Chamber, it is from a distance of seven metres that prehistorians analyse the extraordinary charcoal drawings on a large panel depicting dozens of felines, rhinoceroses and bison. An additional difficulty is the particularly rugged relief of the walls, the presence of alcoves, and natural crevices and folds in the rock, perfectly used by the Aurignacian artists to represent their lexicon of animals, but making the observation and interpretation of the numerous figures problematical. In fact, these are usually deformed when seen from the observer's position. The same holds true for photographs taken facing the walls that can barely render the volume of the animal — lion, bison or horse — especially when it is wrapped around the curve of a rock or disappears into a hidden fold.

Laser scanners record spatial coordinates at 500,000 points per second.

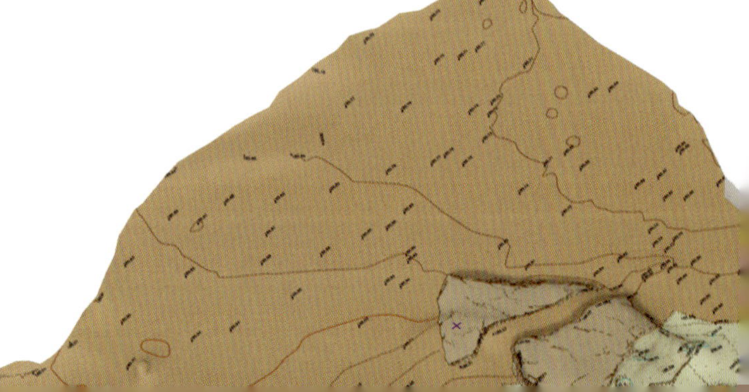

(Knowledge)

Creation of the 3D model of the Chauvet-Pont d'Arc cave and its importance for research.

•

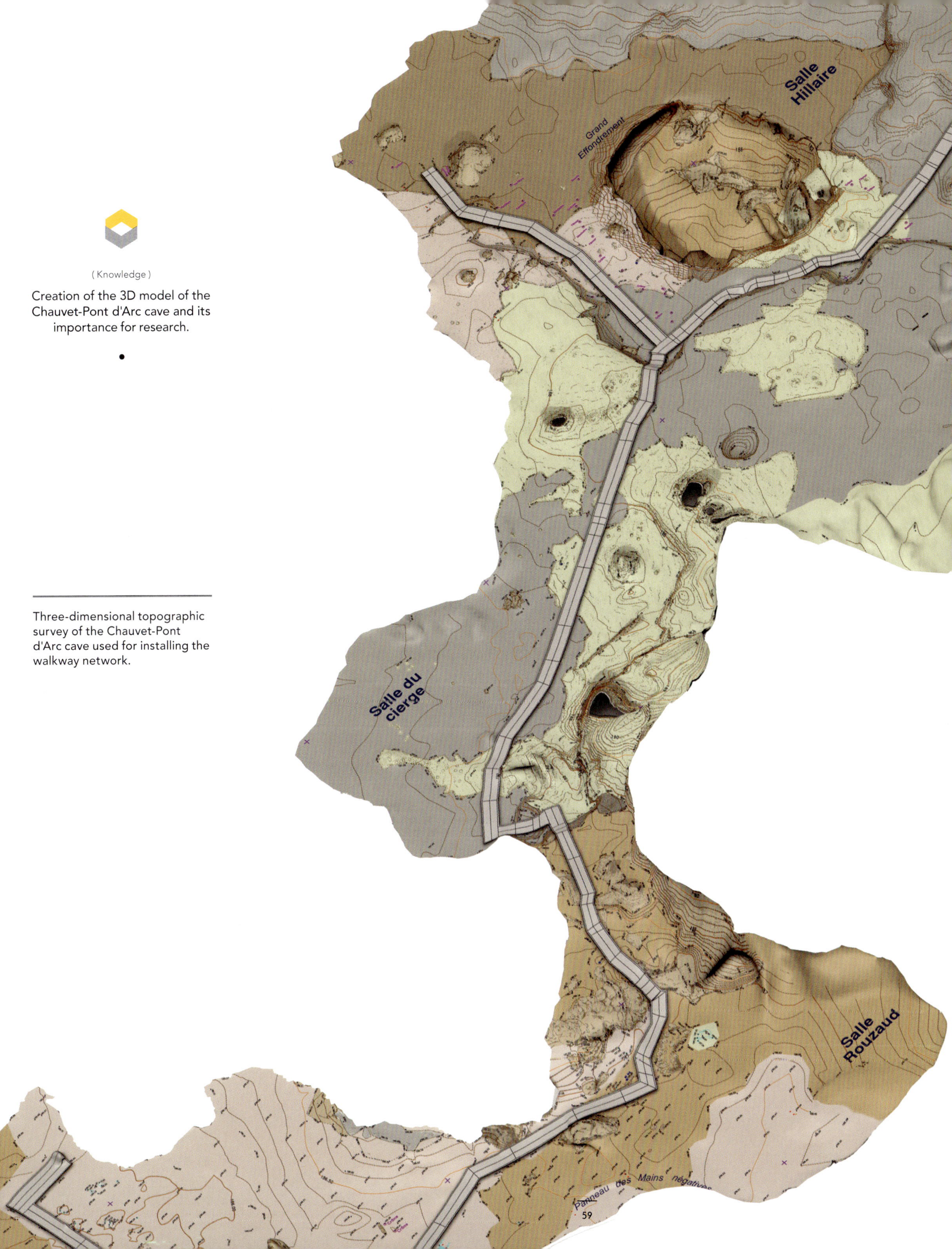

Three-dimensional topographic survey of the Chauvet-Pont d'Arc cave used for installing the walkway network.

To resolve these difficulties, recourse to three-dimensional recording of the volumes, combined with photographs of the paintings and drawings seemed a possible solution. The first trials of this 3D recording technique, initially used in the world of industry, were made by Guy Perazio in 1998 and 1999 in the presence of Jean-Marie Chauvet, in parallel with the installation of the network of walkways and improvements brought to these structures. For this they selected a few figures, in particular two felines in the End Chamber. The method consists of recording with a theodolite, dot by dot, the complex volume of the wall on which the parietal work of art is apposed. Then the photographs of the figures are digitally superimposed on the recording of the volume. A new image in three dimensions containing all the data on the volume and colour of the original wall is obtained in this way. Easily manipulated, this digital image makes it possible to observe the figure from every angle —something impossible inside the cavity— or to virtually light it to reveal the details: lines, brushstrokes, and engravings.

◆

Following the first successful tests, 3D data capture continued with the prehistorian Norbert Aujoulat, a member of the scientific team that studied the Chauvet-Pont d'Arc cave. This researcher, who unfortunately died in 2011, was a pioneer in 3D digital scanning in the underground milieu of decorated caves. In 1994, he had already tested this process (initially developed for the topographical survey of nuclear plants for the French electrical company, EDF) at Vielmouly, a small prehistoric cave in the Dordogne. The scanner has the advantage of simultaneously recording the position of thousands of dots, allowing for greater precision and much higher resolution in the recording of volumes than what can be obtained with a theodolite. The very first 3D surveys in decorated caves date from the 1960s, when France's *Institut géographique national* (National Geographical Institute) made a photogrammetric recording in preparation for the first replica of Lascaux, in the Dordogne.

At Chauvet-Pont d'Arc, Norbert Aujoulat and Guy Perazio developed the method of 3D digitisation on several decorated panels, like that of the Horse traced with the fingers in the Hillaire Chamber, or a black rhinoceros tucked in an alcove in the rock on the side of the large Panel of Horses. Situated far from the walkway, its image seems quite deformed to the observer. But with digitisation, the image of the animal can be straightened on a screen and observed under the same conditions as the Aurignacian artists when they traced it on the wall. As Norbert Aujoulat and Guy Perazio noted, it is the whole of the sanctuary that could be observed in the laboratory in this way, offering the possibility of virtual movement in the cave, the localisation of archaeological evidence, and the highlighting of connections between the various panels. All this, with maximum precision, accurate to one tenth of a millimetre, is made possible by the resolution of the scanner.

In 2010, a new stage in 3D recording was reached. At the request of the Chauvet cave's *Syndicat mixte de l'Espace de restitution*, responsible for the construction of the replica of the cavity planned for 2015, Guy Perazio's team recorded all the volumes of the cavity. In darkness and a silence hardly broken by the sound of water falling drop by drop, the laser scanners recorded the

Guy Perazio, author of the three-dimensional survey of the Chauvet-Pont d'Arc cave, in front of the 3D mesh of the Panel of Lions in the End Chamber.

The geomorphologist Benjamin Sadier, scientific team member, scans the relief of the Cirque d'Estre cliff in order to determine the shape of the original overhang.

3D reconstitution of the overhang forming the entrance to the Chauvet-Pont d'Arc cave as it existed in the Aurignacian period, before it collapsed 21,500 years ago.

spatial coordinates of 500,000 dots per second, more than twenty million for a single decorated wall, and a total of sixteen billion dots for the whole of the cave. Then Lionel Guichard took 6000 high-resolution digital photos, without cast shadows, using calibrated colorimetry, positioned in space, and integrating the bulges and contours of the wall. These photos were then affixed like a digital skin on the scanned volumetric recording.

The 3D model thus obtained constitutes a veritable digital clone of the original cave, an ideal tool for its preservation. By eliminating the necessity for entering the cave, researchers are able to make a precise study of the paintings and drawings on a screen, take measurements, and analyse the various lines and strokes. They can also employ raking light to make the delicate engravings traced in flint by the artists stand out, or employ flickering light such as the artist used to light his work 36,000 years ago.

(Animation)

3D reconstitution of the original overhang of the Chauvet-Pont d'Arc cave and its closing.

If 3D imaging makes it possible to reveal the beauty and perfection of parietal artworks, it is equally precious for understanding the geological history of the cavity. In this way, geomorphologists have been able to describe and date the events that led to the closing of the overhang at the mouth of the cave that collapsed after the artists' passage. For this, the researcher Benjamin Sadier of the University of Savoy's EDYTEM Laboratory (France) first made a digital study of the cliff overlooking the cavity. Then he took the measurements of the rocks that had rolled down below the cave as well as those in scree left from the collapse of the overhang, visible in the first chamber of the cavity. By virtually replacing the volume of rock detached from the wall on the cliff (about 4,500 cubic metres), he was able to reconstitute the shape and size of the original overhang: ten metres high and twelve wide. It was also possible to situate the rockslide that occurred in several stages in time: the last of them 21,500 years ago, using samples of rocks on the cliff, dated through the analysis of an isotope of chlorine (^{36}Cl).

The Cave's Geological Secrets Unveiled

Inside the cavity, digitisation also makes it possible to understand how — and eventually why — humans arranged the cave in conjunction with their artistic practices. Piles of rocks, steps ostensibly carved in the clay, and the presence of strange water retention basins were some of the things that intrigued the geomorphologists. The scanner enabled them to study these vestiges from a distance without damaging them. Through analysis of the images, they were able to pierce some of the most disturbing secrets of the amazing Chauvet-Pont d'Arc cave. A cave that continues to surprise and astound us.

THREE STEPS IN 3D DIGITALISATION

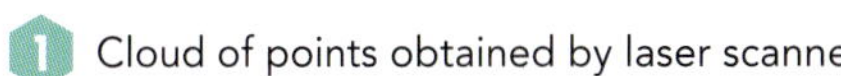
1. Cloud of points obtained by laser scanner.

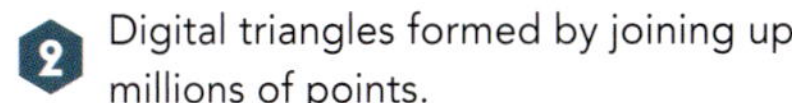
2. Digital triangles formed by joining up millions of points.

3. Texturing by superposition of photographs on the "digital skin".

(following pages)
Three steps in 3D digitalisation of the Chauvet-Pont d'Arc cave. Here, the End Chamber.

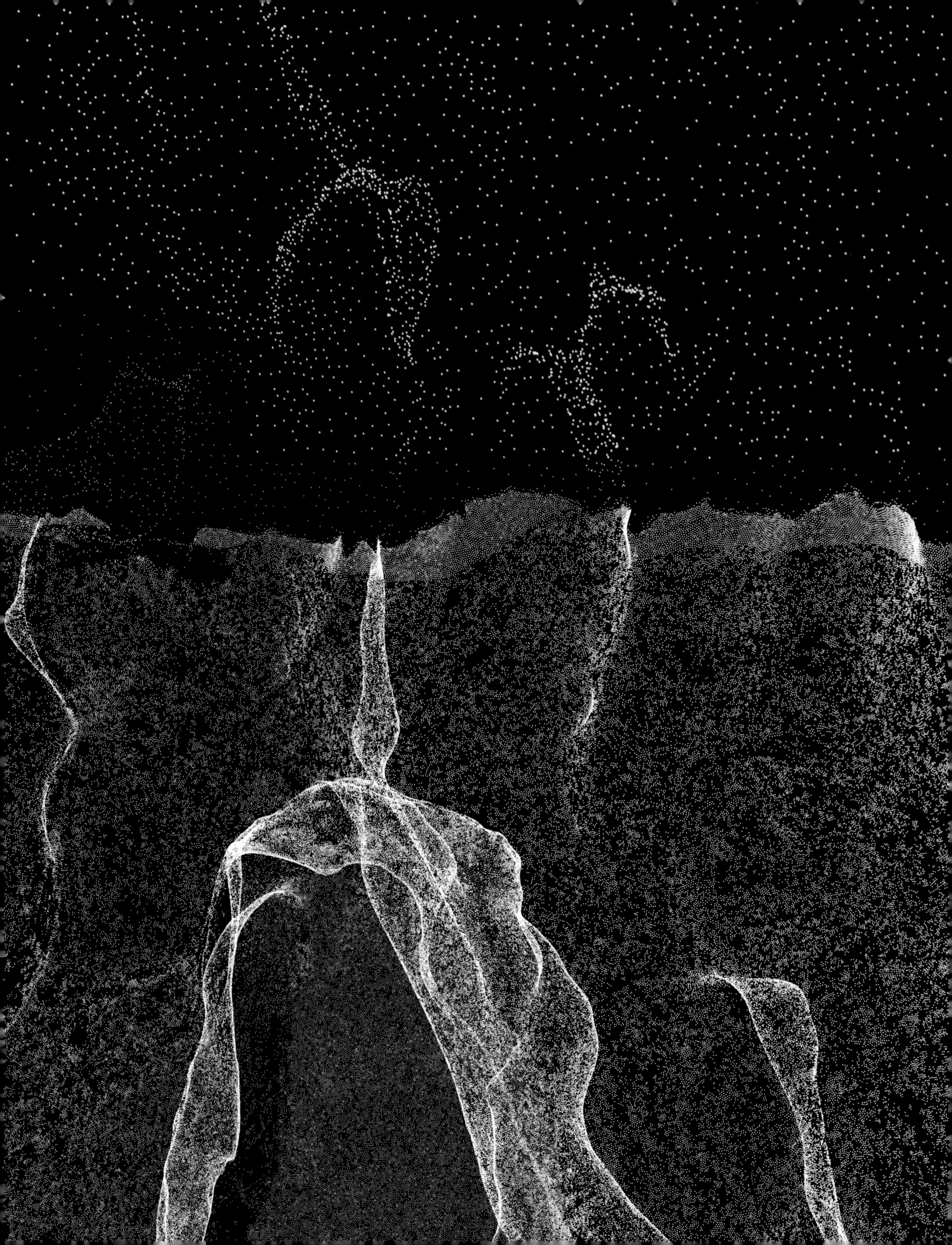

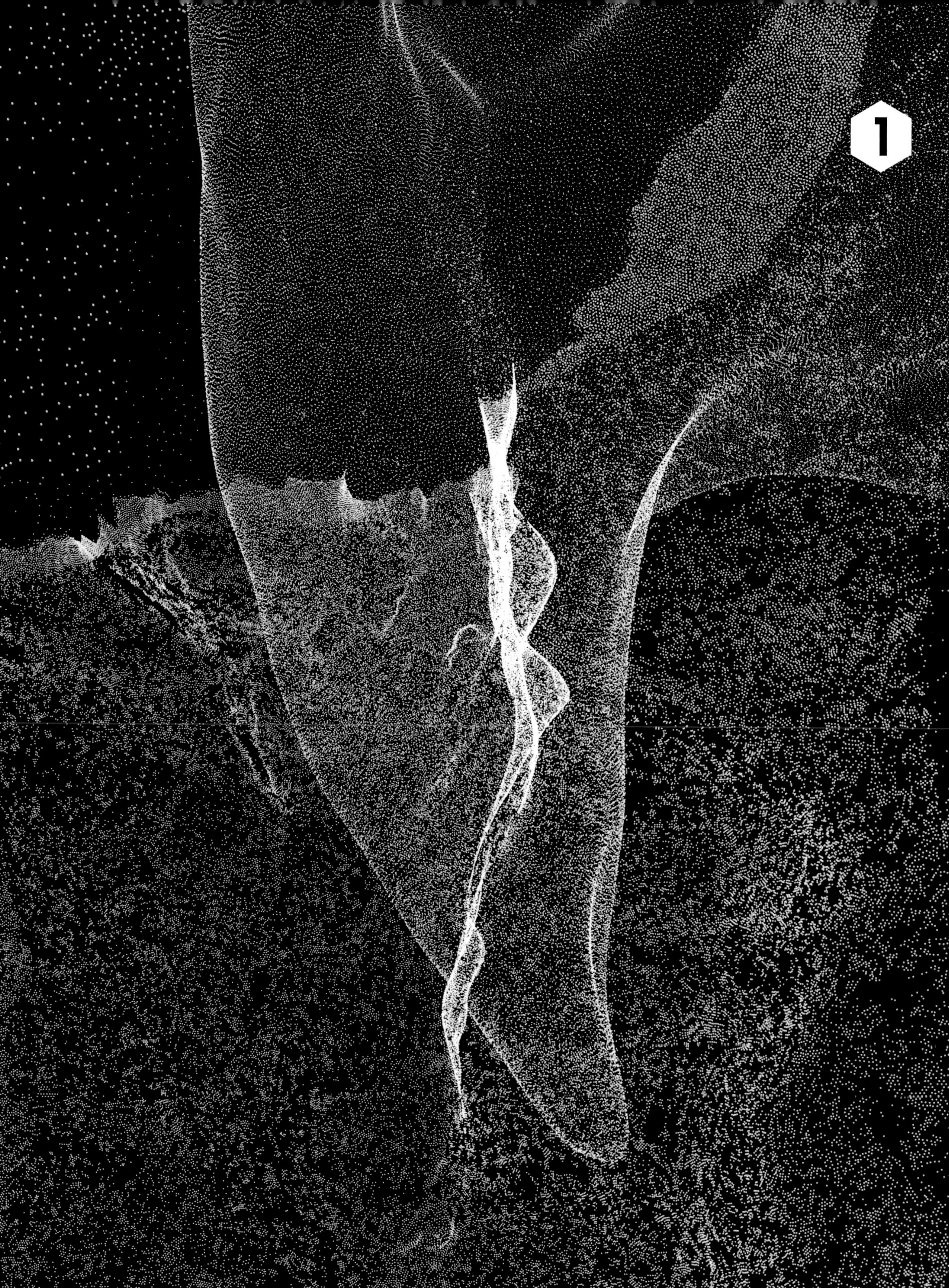
1

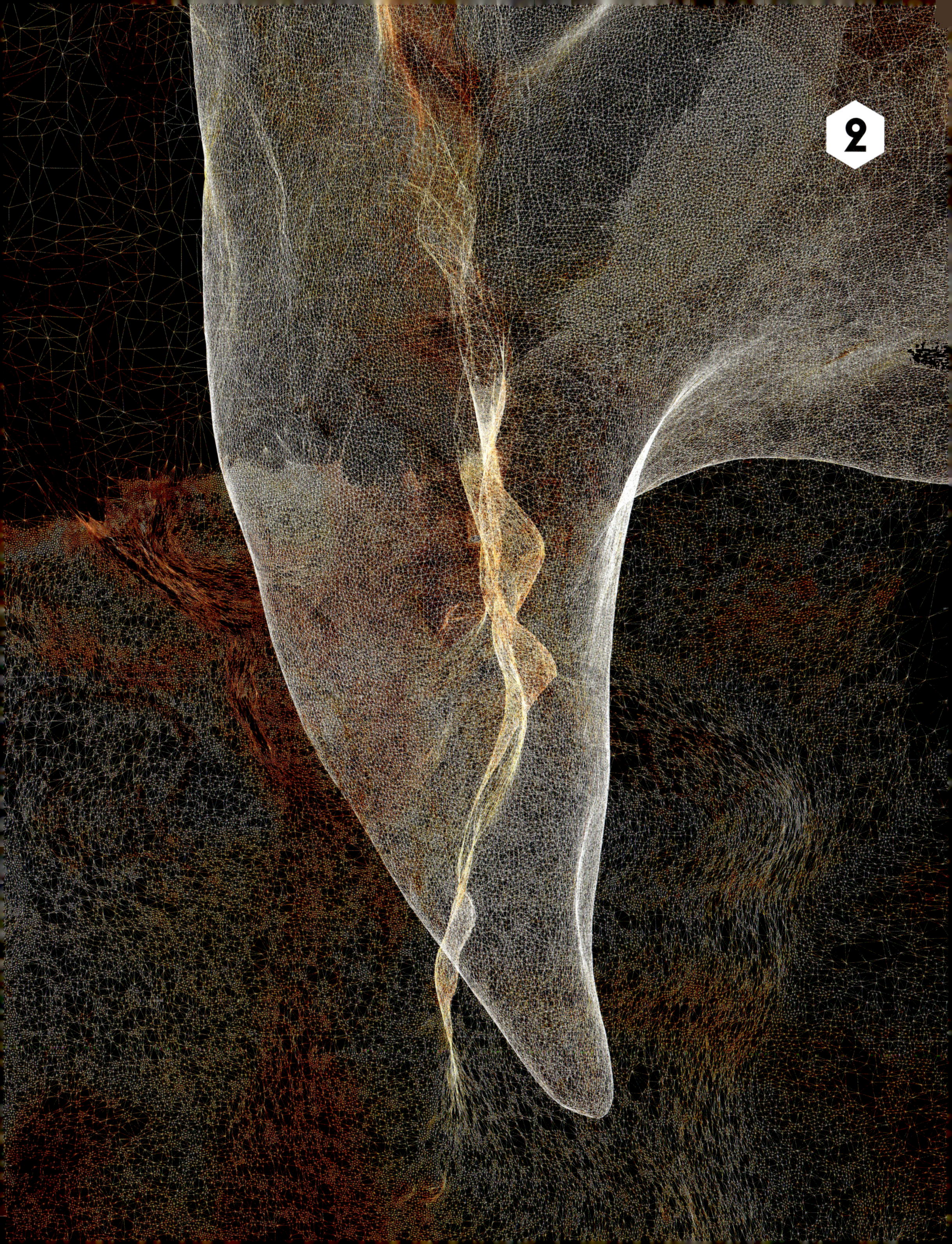
2

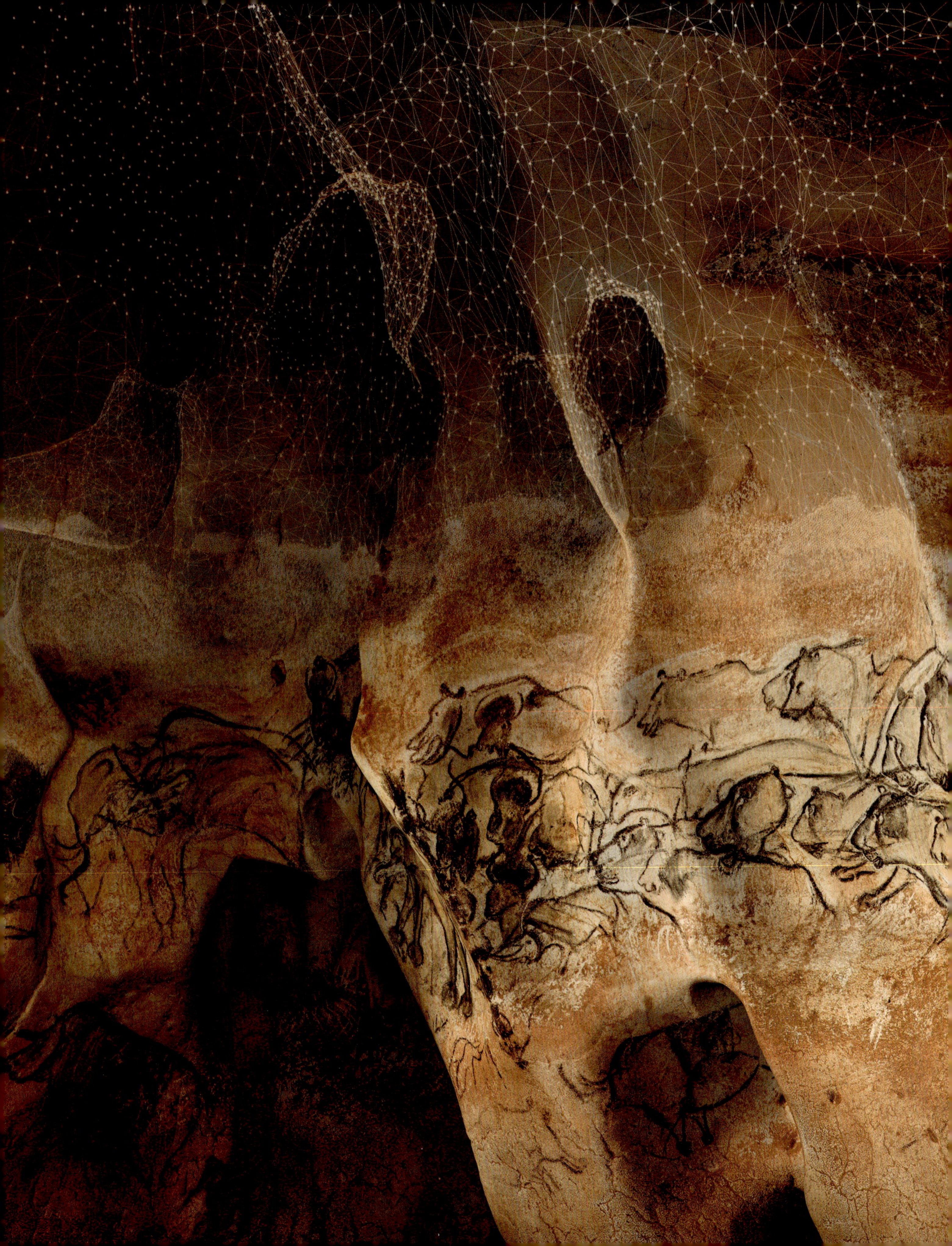

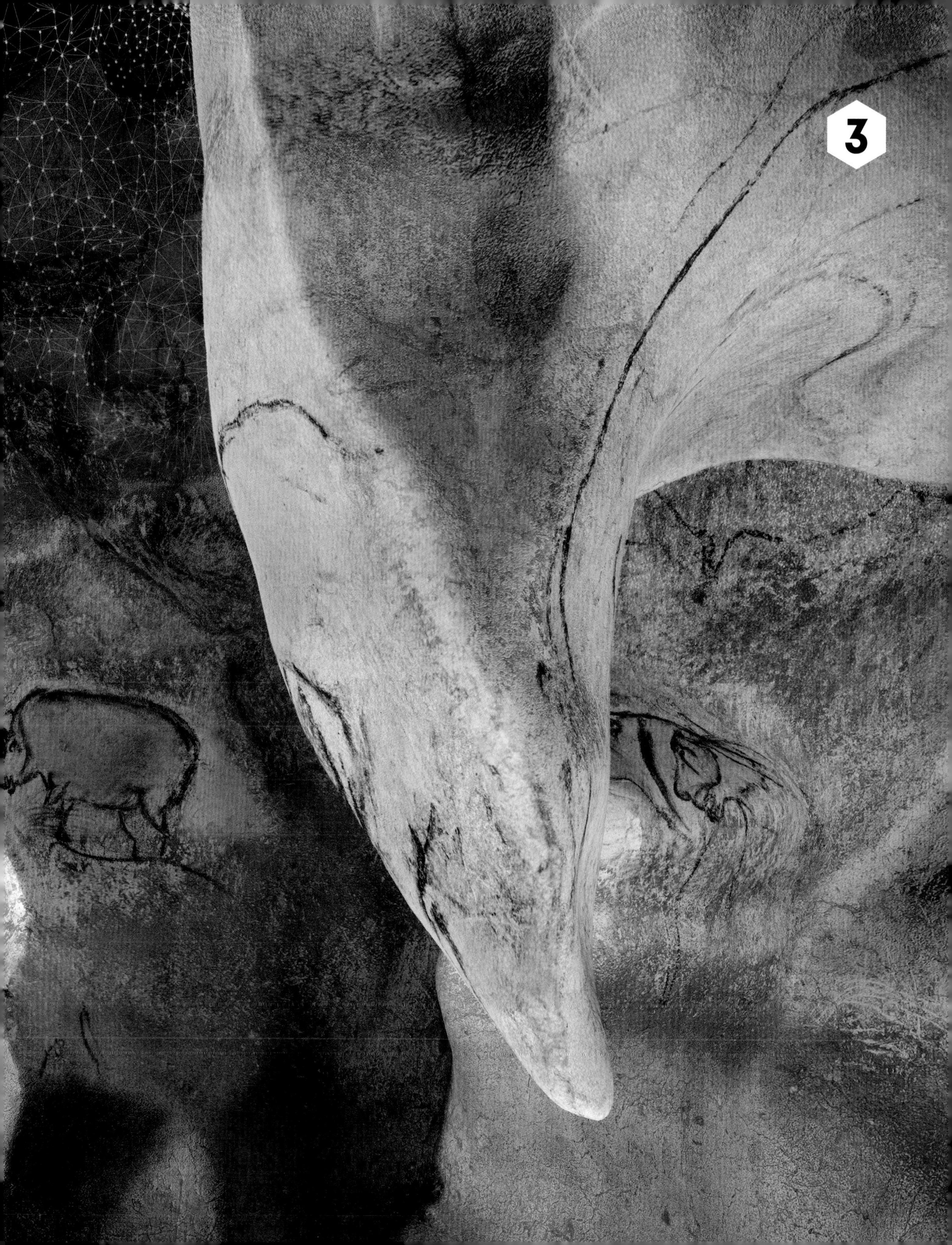
3

04

THE CAVE THAT CHANGED EVERYTHING

The beginnings of our humanity

The Chauvet-Pont d'Arc cave has reached us intact, and since its discovery it has never stopped stupefying scientists and its rare visitors. The main reason for this fascination is the surpassing beauty of the painted figures it contains, in particular 442 animal representations displaying an incredible technical mastery. But beyond these masterpieces that possess the power of conveying profound emotion to the viewer, it is the cavity itself, totally occupied and sanctified 36,000 years ago, which upsets all our ideas about the origins of art and our cultural beginnings.

The weeks following its exploration, the Chauvet-Pont d'Arc cave was recognised as a major discovery, due to its fabulous artistic and archaeological vestiges and its excellent state of conservation. During his first visits, the prehistorian Jean Clottes noted the presence of hundreds of cave bear skeletal remains, numerous pieces of charcoal and a dozen flints on the ground. On the walls, decorated with hundreds of signs and animals, the specialist identified two categories of figures, red and black, and a bestiary largely dominated by dangerous animals: rhinoceroses, lions and mammoths. The techniques employed immediately pointed to talent worthy of the great masters of Prehistory, and beyond. In their representations of the animals observed in the wild, they demonstrate a perfect command of drawing, painting, engraving and stumping, as well as a masterly use of the uneven contours of the walls.

Already in 1995, all these treasures placed Chauvet-Pont d'Arc in the pantheon of Palaeolithic decorated caves, alongside Lascaux in Dordogne, Niaux in Ariège, Cosquer in Provence or Altamira in Spain.

At the time, the Ardèche cavity represented the latest discovery to date in European Palaeolithic cave art, a cultural practice that persisted in Europe, underground for the most part, between 36,000 and 10,000 years ago during the Aurignacian, Gravettian, Solutrean and Magdalenian periods. According to prehistorians, decorated caves were sanctuaries reserved for ritual practices: initiation ceremonies, shamanic rites or the transmission of mythology. They are mostly decorated with animal figures often depicted in profile, without natural elements, vegetation or relief, as well as numerous handprints, mysterious signs and half-human, half-animal forms.

The techniques employed point to talent worthy of the great masters of Prehistory, and beyond.

The artists represented a figure associating legs and a female sex with a bison and a feline on this hanging rock in the End Chamber.

A Particularly Dangerous Bestiary

Following these first observations, the scientific study of Chauvet-Pont d'Arc begun in 1998 only confirmed its incomparable richness. In total, more than 1,000 figures were counted on the walls, of which 442 are representations of animals, numerous signs (dots, lines, schematic hatches and "W" signs), as well as human figurations: positive and negative hands, vulvas and a disturbing pair of female legs associated with a pubic triangle, executed on a hanging rock in the last chamber of the cave.

But beyond the numbers, the type of bestiary represented at Chauvet-Pont d'Arc, in addition to the very great age of the figures and their remarkable technical mastery, make the Ardèche cave a major prehistoric site. Here the painters chose to represent essentially dangerous animals, impressive by their physical strength and their courage. It must be noted that these were not animals that they hunted. Thus the big cat-mammoth-rhinoceros triad largely dominates the bestiary, totaling half the animals that figure in the cave. The cave lion is the most often depicted with 80 representations, just before the mammoth (79) and the woolly rhinoceros (72), followed far behind by the horse, numbering 52. The big cats of Chauvet-Pont d'Arc alone represent 61% of all those recorded in European cave art, a proportion that reaches almost 75% for the rhinoceros.

With this dangerous, even threatening animal lexicon, Chauvet-Pont d'Arc differs from the later sanctuaries — from the Gravettian period onwards (see chronology page 29) — where more peaceful species are dominant: horses, stags or ibexes. For researchers, this deliberate choice corresponds to the nature of the myths and complex beliefs that the Aurignacian

A FABULOUS BESTIARY COMES OUT OF THE SHADOWS

Fourteen or fifteen animal species that lived in the Ardèche during the ice age are represented on the walls of the Chauvet-Pont d'Arc cave. These are largely dominated by dangerous species that were not hunted. In total, 442 animals are depicted, of which 61 are indeterminate.

Estimated Total Number of Figures on the Walls: Approximately 1,000

WOOLLY RHINOCEROS
Coelodonta antiquitatis
72

HORSE
Equus caballus
52

BISON
Bison priscus
30

CAVE BEAR
Ursus spelaeus
19

IBEX
Capra ibex
17

REINDEER
Rangifer tarandus
13

AUROCHS
Bos primigenius
8

MEGALOCEROS
Megaloceros giganteus
5

STAG
Cervus elaphus
2

MUSK OX
Ovibos moschatus
2

PANTHER
Panthera spelaea
1

HYENA
Crocuta crocuta
1?

OWL
Bubo bubo
1

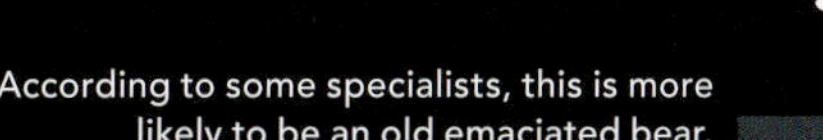

According to some specialists, this is more likely to be an old emaciated bear.

painters projected on the walls. The founding myths that find their illustration in cave art must have been peopled with such beasts, which were both powerful and feared. We see that their descendants, at Lascaux for instance, favoured less bellicose animals.

The Chauvet-Pont d'Arc animal lexicon is also characterized by great diversity; the greatest to be found in all cave art, with fifteen species depicted. Besides the four already mentioned, we find the bison, the cave bear, the aurochs, the ibex, the reindeer, the stag, the megaloceros stag, the musk ox, the panther, the owl and the hyena. Even though it is possible that the image of the latter may in fact correspond to an emaciated bear, perhaps at the end of hibernation.

To represent this symbolic animal pantheon, the Chauvet-Pont d'Arc artists possessed a sophisticated panoply of techniques that still leaves the specialists of cave art and all those who have observed their work dumbfounded: drawings in charcoal, red and yellow ochre paintings, swabs or the palm of the hand used to apply pigment to the walls, delicate engraving with flint or the fingers when the support was soft enough, preparation of the wall by scraping the soft surface, use of the contours of the rock to represent the animals, stumping to further accentuate the volume of their bodies, representation of movement, suggestion of perspective.

In addition, some techniques have been used in combination to create some of the most beautiful masterpieces of Palaeolithic art, and of art in general. This is the case in the Panel of Horses in the Hillaire Chamber, which stunningly associates drawing, engraving and stumping to compose a complex fresco featuring horses, aurochs and rhinoceroses. Or the final scene presented to the visitor in the depths of the cavity, that gem of Palaeolithic art: lions attacking a herd of bison. Our admiration and emotion reach great heights before these elaborate pictures, wonderfully preserved, in which dozens of animals that seem vibrant with life are combined in veritable ethological scenes: a great cat, recognisable as a male by his scrotum, in a mating dance; two bellicose, rutting rhinoceroses in confrontation; or patient, silently stalking lions before the final attack.

For prehistorians, the shock felt at Chauvet-Pont d'Arc was even greater since the awe-inspiring, prodigiously executed drawings inside the cavity are also the oldest know to us: 36,000 years. The dating of samples taken from the cavity — 85 in all — confirms this. These tests have revealed two stages of occupation of the site, the oldest of them dating to circa -36,000 during the Aurignacian period, and the second circa -30,000 during the Gravettian period. But it seems that only the Aurignacians executed the paintings and drawings. Their much later successors spent time there, ostensibly impressed by what they saw, but it is probable that they did not leave any artistic trace.

However, the theories inherited from the work of the French prehistorian and ethnologist André Leroi-Gourhan in the 1960s were based on the assumption that Palaeolithic cave art began with imperfect, fledgling forms during the Aurignacian period, then improved and developed little by little in the course of many thousands of years, until it culminated in the sublime Lascaux of the Magdalenian period. With Chauvet-Pont d'Arc, this gradualist conception of the origins and evolution of art was entirely upset and rejected. To the contrary, in the Ardèche cavity, the art of the earliest times is perfectly mastered from the very

A STRANGE HUMAN PRESENCE

Beside the very numerous animal figures and signs, the Aurignacian artists also represented themselves. They did so in a stylised manner, selecting certain very characteristic parts of their anatomy: hands, vulvas and female legs. These first known representations of *Homo sapiens* raise questions among researchers: why did they make these choices? Why didn't they draw faces, whereas they could have without difficulty? This remains a mystery.

FEMALE LEGS WITH PUBIC TRIANGLE

↑

Two female legs combined with a pubic triangle were traced in charcoal on a rock pendant in the End Chamber. A stupefying prehistoric Venus, whose deeper meaning escapes us.

VULVAS

←

Drawn in charcoal or engraved using the finger tracing technique.

Total number: 6

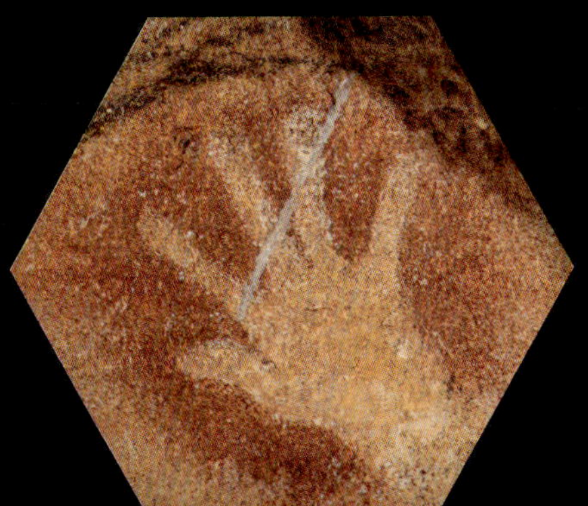

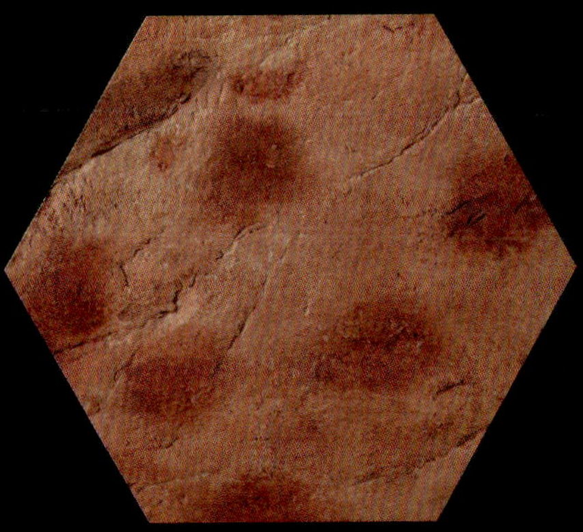

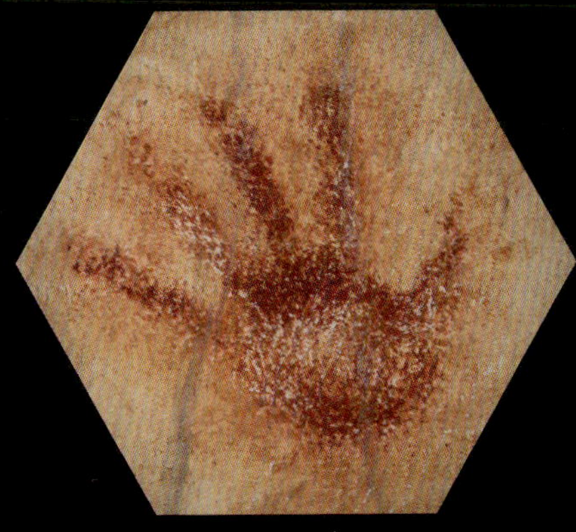

NEGATIVE HANDS

Obtained by placing the hand on the wall and spitting ochre on it with the mouth, resulting in a negative form using the stencil technique.

Total number: 5

PALMS OF THE HAND

Obtained by applying the palm of the hand covered in ochre on the wall, either in an isolated way or combining several dots to form a figure.

Number: approximately 500

POSITIVE HANDS

Obtained by applying the whole hand covered in ochre on the wall.

Total number: 7

start. Another theory overturned due to Chauvet-Pont d'Arc: the zone of influence of Palaeolithic cave art, until then centred on the French-Cantabria region (Dordogne, Pyrenees, Pays Basque and Cantabria) overlaps largely to the east, with the Ardèche becoming the next major centre of prehistoric art in the same way as Provence with Cosquer, or the Yonne with Arcy-sur-Cure.

With Chauvet-Pont d'Arc, the gradualist conception of the evolution of art was entirely upset.

It is probable that there were only a few masters working at Chauvet-Pont d'Arc, as suggested by certain graphic codes that the specialists have identified in several parts of the cave. This is what the prehistorian and artist responsible for the study of art of the earliest times as well as its reproduction for the replica of Chauvet-Pont d'Arc, Gilles Tosello believes. Thus the very characteristic way of representing the ears of the rhinoceroses, on both sides of the line forming the back, or the very marked "frontal stop" of the cave bears, that is to say the angle formed by the muzzle and the brow, are found throughout the decorated chambers.

A single master painter may have supervised this limited number of artists. In order to prepare their pigments, and specifically charcoal, the artists burned branches of Scots pine, especially in the deeper areas of the cavity. However there is no evidence of this activity in the End Chamber, one of the most richly decorated, conceivably to avoid filling it with smoke. Once their charcoal crayons were ready, the artists' quick sure strokes brought the lions, aurochs and horses to life on the walls. These beasts look to the visitor as though they are lying in wait in the shadows of the chambers until the guide's torch illuminates them.

Does the emergence of art at Chauvet-Pont d'Arc mean that it suddenly appeared, invented by geniuses endowed with intelligence and a command of techniques that broke with the *Homo sapiens* preceding them? Certainly not. Chauvet-Pont d'Arc did not erupt from nothingness. Previous artistic forms certainly existed, perhaps in other undiscovered cavities or on perishable supports such as skin, bark or walls exposed to the elements. Moreover, Chauvet-Pont d'Arc is not completely alone at the beginnings of Palaeolithic cave art. Other decorated sites have been dated at the same time: Deux-Ouvertures, Tête du Lion and the Grotte aux Points in the Ardèche, the Castanet Rock Shelter in Dordogne, Baume Latrone in the Gard and Coliboaia in Rumania. In addition, in these two last caves we find bestiaries composed of felines, mammoths and rhinoceroses similar to that found at Chauvet-Pont d'Arc. This cultural proximity is reinforced by convergences in style in Coliboaia and the Ardèche: the same way of representing the ears of the rhinoceros using a comma on both sides of the line forming the back, for example. So it is a veritable European culture that emerges at the dawn of the occupation of this continent by *Homo sapiens*, invented and imported by nomadic tribes of hunter-gatherers coming from the east of the continent, Eurasia and the Near East. Little by little these nomads colonised the whole of Europe, bringing with them their beliefs, their techniques and their social organisation. After choosing this site fashioned by natural elements considered as deities, they created their most breathtaking masterpiece at Chauvet-Pont d'Arc.

Like their peers in other regions, the Chauvet-Pont d'Arc artists respected certain stylistic conventions, possibly consisting of some sort of control exercised by the rest of the group over the general form of animals and the manner of representing their eyes, ears and limbs. Nevertheless, the artists who decorated the Chauvet-Pont d'Arc cave also expressed great creativity and freedom in their drawing, along with a wholly uncommon capacity for observation and imitation. According to the prehistorian and member of the scientific team, Valérie Feruglio, in order to draw certain anatomical details of the limbs, the head or the breast with such precision, it is probable that the Aurignacians observed their models in the wild at length before painting them. It is even conceivable that they practised the equivalent of dissection on the animals they hunted or found dead.

Once it came to recreating these creatures inside the cavity, freed from certain graphic conventions and that *"Aurignacian cultural immersion"* proposed by Valérie Feruglio, they granted themselves *"veritable creative freedom"* with their work in the secrecy of the sanctuary.

Artists playing both a spiritual role for the group and creators in their own right, the Chauvet-Pont d'Arc painters occupied the whole of the cavity, taking turns with the hibernating cave bears, as suggested by the claw marks superimposed on certain drawings. Evidence of human presence has been found in the smallest recesses of the cavity, even the undecorated areas. Thus in the Gallery of Crosshatches, more than 200 metres from the entrance, a child's footprints were discovered, touching proof of exploration that may have happened 36,000 years ago in the Aurignacian period, or more recently during a second human intrusion. This human presence is especially disturbing when we are faced with figures that are so fresh that they seem to have been drawn the day before. Or when we witness those touching handprints on the rock, negative and positive palms or whole hands. Scientific study has shown that some were a woman's or an adolescent's hands (is it the same person in the Gallery of Crosshatches?) Or when others found in several places in the cavity belonged to a tall man, about 1.8 metres in height, with a slightly crooked little finger. This is the incomparable magic of Chauvet-Pont d'Arc where *Homo sapiens* seems always to be there, on the ground and on the walls, in all his humanness.

A Methodically Organised Underground Space

Another remarkable result of scientific study is the clear division brought to light between the initial zone of the cave, before a threshold marked by a narrowing of the cavity, and its deepest chambers. The first area is decorated mostly with red paintings, palm prints on the walls or animal figures. A little further on these same Aurignacian artists, or others belonging to the same group, primarily made drawings in charcoal, organised in very complex panels and compositions, as well as engravings. At Chauvet-Pont d'Arc, it was therefore the underground space as a whole that was occupied, explored and then structured through the choice of colours, animal themes and degrees of complexity in the works. These options were not left to chance, and may have corresponded to the various cycles in the tales and myths recounted on the walls, or the rituals that members of the group performed before the works. And what is the meaning of the two bear humeri stuck in the loamy soil close to the original entrance? Were they symbolic markers to indicate the entrance to the sanctuary? This is one possibility.

A PARTICULARLY RICH RANGE OF TECHNIQUES

To create their masterpiece the Aurignacian artists of Chauvet-Pont d'Arc used nine elaborate graphic techniques, often together, which make them accomplished prehistoric masters, and masters in the history of art.

ENGRAVING

More or less delicate, it was done with a hard instrument in stone, bone or wood or with flint points. Here, a feline engraved on the panel facing right in the End Chamber.

PAINTING

The pigment, mostly red ochre (rarely yellow), was applied to the wall by blowing, or using the fingers, a swab or a brush, as seen with this big cat and this mammoth in the Panel of Red Signs.

STOMP

By spreading the pulverulent charcoal pigment on the soft whitish support of the wall, the artists obtained shades of gray capable of rendering an animal's shape. Rhinoceros in the monumental Panel of Lions in the End Chamber.

DRAWING

The pigment, charcoal obtained by burning Scots pine, was applied to the wall with the fingers or with crayons. It is this technique among others that was employed for the rhinoceros situated in the End Chamber.

(Knowledge)

Techniques employed by the Chauvet-Pont d'Arc artists.

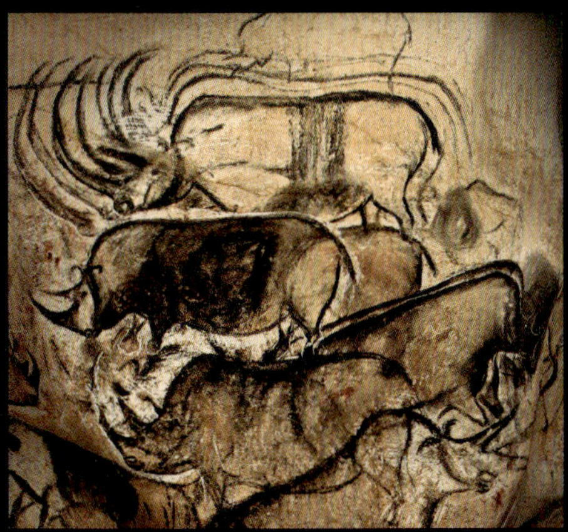

PERSPECTIVE

By repeating certain anatomical parts of the animals, for example the horns of the rhinoceros, the artists transcribed the notion of perspective, as they visually experienced it when observing animals outside. Rhinoceros on the monumental Panel of Lions in the End Chamber.

REPRESENTATION OF MOVEMENT

The animals are sometimes represented in movement, or integrated into veritable ethological scenes, like these two attacking lions in the Panel of Lions in the End Chamber.

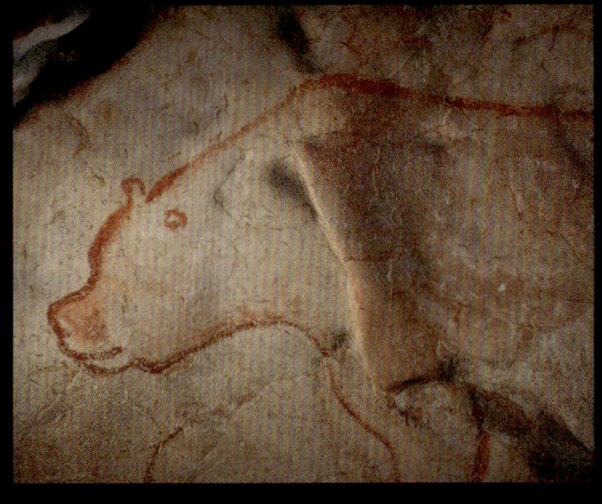

USE OF CONTOURS

The artists integrated the forms and contours of the wall to bring out certain anatomical details of the animals, such as this cave bear's back in the Bear Passage.

FINGER TRACING

This technique consisted of removing the soft matter on the surface of the wall by passing the fingers over it to reveal the colour underneath, as seen in this horse in the Hillaire Chamber.

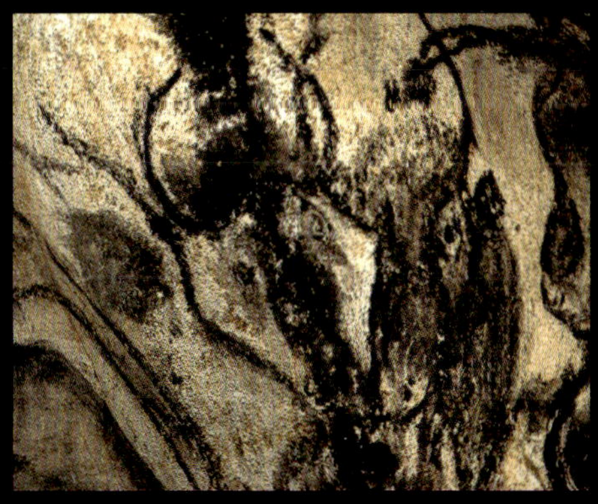

THREE-DIMENSIONAL REPRESENTATION

Some animals are represented in three planes in space, with a consummate use of relief, like this head of a bison depicted frontally and in two profiles in the End Chamber.

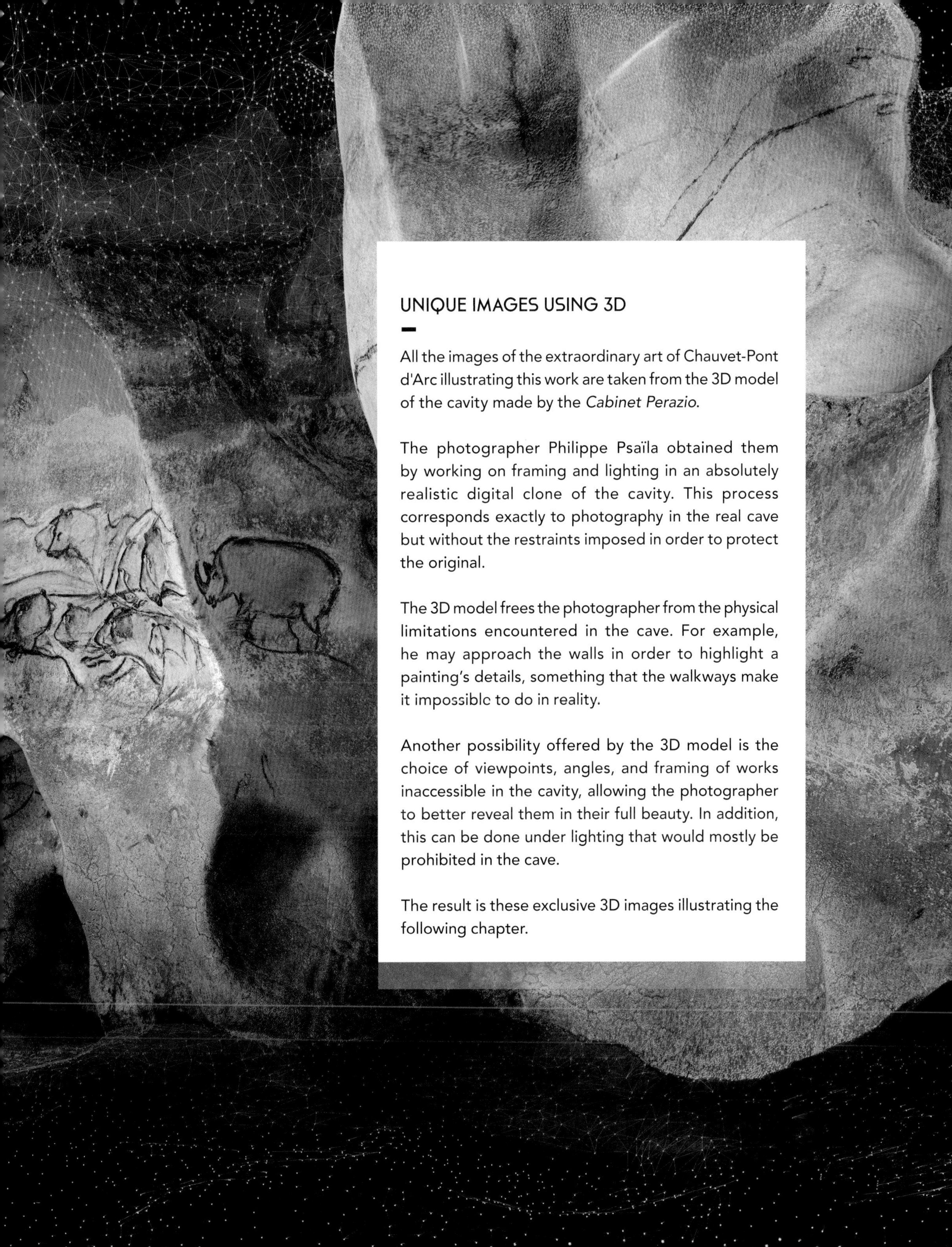

UNIQUE IMAGES USING 3D

All the images of the extraordinary art of Chauvet-Pont d'Arc illustrating this work are taken from the 3D model of the cavity made by the *Cabinet Perazio*.

The photographer Philippe Psaïla obtained them by working on framing and lighting in an absolutely realistic digital clone of the cavity. This process corresponds exactly to photography in the real cave but without the restraints imposed in order to protect the original.

The 3D model frees the photographer from the physical limitations encountered in the cave. For example, he may approach the walls in order to highlight a painting's details, something that the walkways make it impossible to do in reality.

Another possibility offered by the 3D model is the choice of viewpoints, angles, and framing of works inaccessible in the cavity, allowing the photographer to better reveal them in their full beauty. In addition, this can be done under lighting that would mostly be prohibited in the cave.

The result is these exclusive 3D images illustrating the following chapter.

05

THE CHAUVET-PONT D'ARC CAVE REVEALED

A visit to the main decorated chambers of the Aurignacian sanctuary, with images from the 3D model.

BRUNEL CHAMBER

The Brunel Chamber is the first one we enter after descending the metal ladder once past the airlock at the cave's entrance. What strikes us first is the immensity of the volumes and its mineralogical beauty. On the west side, scree obstructing the original entrance to the cavity is clearly visible. The five groups of figures in this first area are evenly divided on the walls, and distributed around a mass of rocks formed by blocks fallen from the vault and limestone concretions.

Here prehistoric humans covered their hands in red ochre and applied the palms to form the shape of animals as seen in the large Dotted Animal Panel, or mysterious symbolic figures as in the Panel of the Sacred Heart. They also entered a narrow passage hidden from the chamber to paint three cave bears that give the impression of springing from the bowels of the earth, creating a picture full of respect for a mighty animal ostensibly admired by the painters. Like the majority of figures in this first area of the cavity, those in the Brunel Chamber are executed in red ochre, although the only yellow paintings in Chauvet-Pont d'Arc are to be found in a little alcove here: two small horses, reduced to their heads, accompanied by red signs.

(Exploration)

The Vestibule of Red Bears.

(opposite)
In the Vestibule of Red Bears, the artists represented three cave bears in red ochre, such as these two, perhaps an adult and a younger bear. Bears occupied the cavern more than half the year to hibernate and humans vacated it during those periods.

(following pages)
Painted at the end of the vestibule, the third bear springs from a hollow in the rock that replaces its hindquarters, as described by Dominique Baffier and Valérie Feruglio, the prehistorians studying the cave art in the Brunel Chamber.

When they painted the bears in the vestibule in torchlight, the artists were crouching in an uncomfortable position facing the wall. Their pictorial prowess thus forces even greater admiration, as does the effect of staging achieved by the painters.

On the right panel of the Vestibule of Red Bears, an ibex is traced in red ochre. The artist made intelligent use of the relief and irregularities in the wall in its representation. Thus fissures in the rock, which pre-existed the work, embody the two horns and part of the dorsal line. Another smaller ibex is painted under the first one.

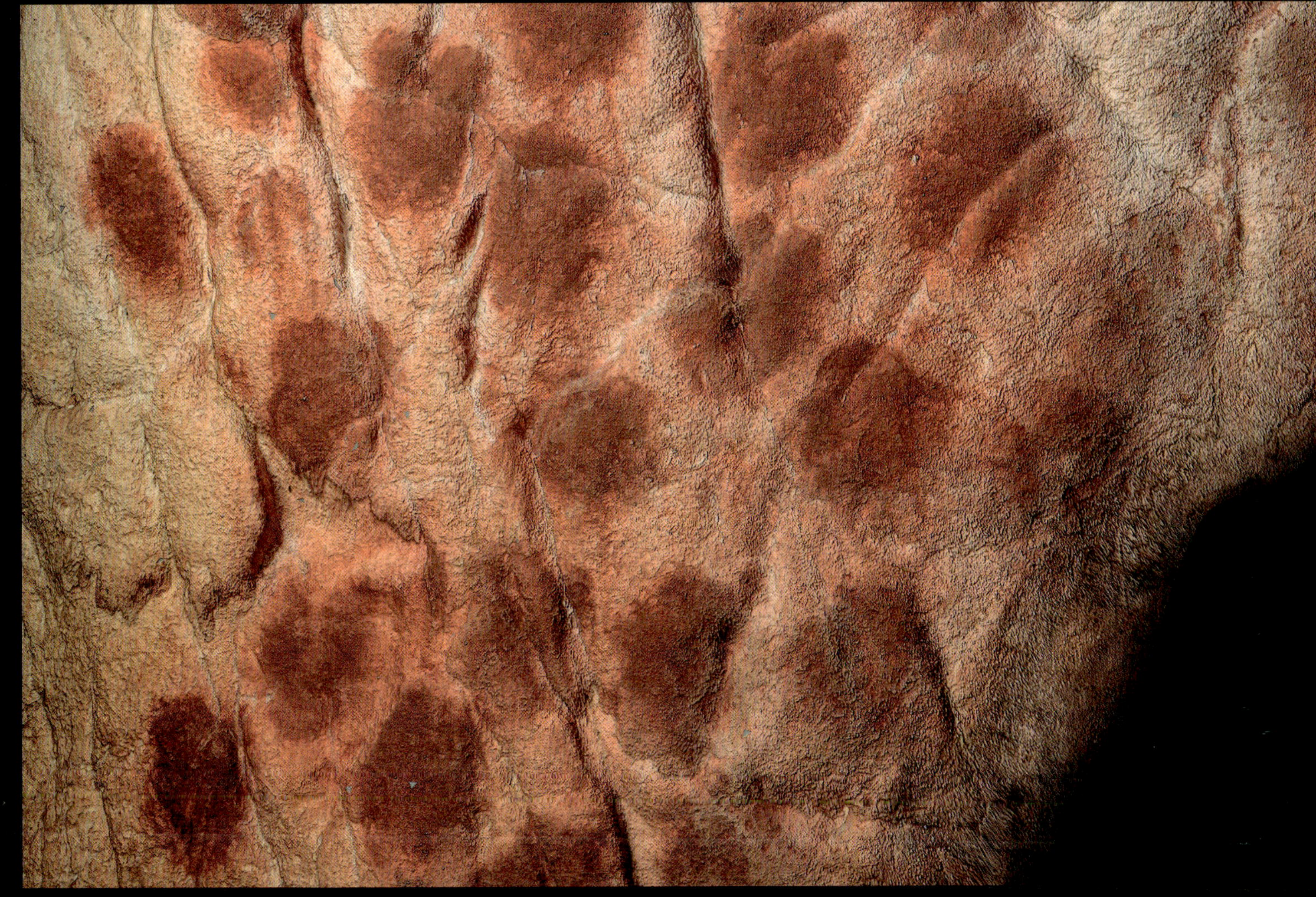

When studying, among others, this hanging rock decorated with red dots, the researchers showed that at least two people placed the palms of their hands on the walls of the Brunel Chamber: a man almost six feet tall and a woman or an adolescent. Left of the panel: a complete handprint is visible, with two fingers joined.

RED PANELS CHAMBER

After crossing the vast Chamber of the Bear Hollows, almost devoid of paintings, where the floor retains traces of the hibernation of bears as well as their paw prints, we turn toward the Red Panels Chamber, the last one before the threshold marking the passage to the area of black drawings. Here too the artists mostly used red ochre for their paintings, including a panel composed of several rhinoceroses, hands and signs, and a snow leopard with a spotted chest. This work alone, according to the specialist Jean Clottes, is enough to ensure the renown of the Ardèche cavity. In fact, the snow leopard is exceptional in Palaeolithic parietal art.

Four important panels are to be found in this chamber: the Panels of the Panther (the only one on the left wall), Red Signs, Positive Hands and Negative Hands, this last accompanied by a small bear in the background. The prehistorians Norbert Aujoulat, Carole Fritz and Gilles Tosello who have extensively studied the parietal art in this chamber, explain the distribution of the panels by the necessity to take into account the rugged rock medium, with the imposing presence of a stalagmite cascade. The Panel of Red Signs is also characterised by representations of insects, butterflies and centipedes, or in any case, figures that may be interpreted as such. Although according to scientists, they may in fact be abstract signs, simply evoking animal shapes, wings or legs. Whatever their precise meaning, these figures further contribute to the enigmatic nature, almost impenetrable to us, of the art of Chauvet-Pont d'Arc. Art that is at once realistic yet filled with symbols, which fundamentally remains a mystery. Could the Aurignacians have used this area of the sanctuary, which prepares for the breathtaking drawings and engravings in the next chambers, to record coded messages whose meaning now escapes us?

(opposite)
On this hanging rock, two figures with a shape suggesting a bird with spread wings, or a butterfly, were painted in red ochre. Are they symbols, abstract signs or animal depictions?

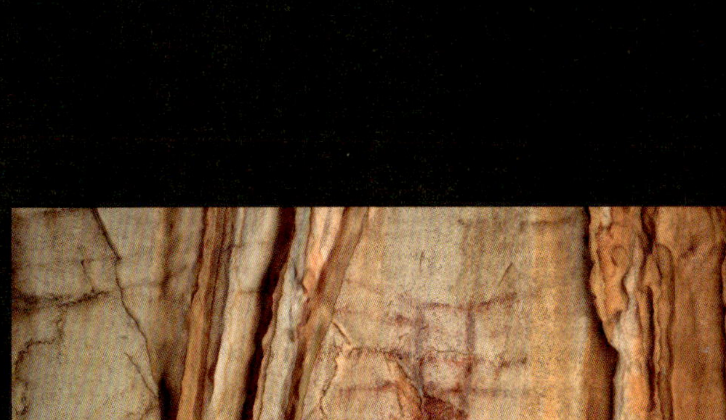

(opposite, from top to bottom)
Other examples of figures suggesting the general shape of insects: this "spider" or "centipede" represented between two limestone

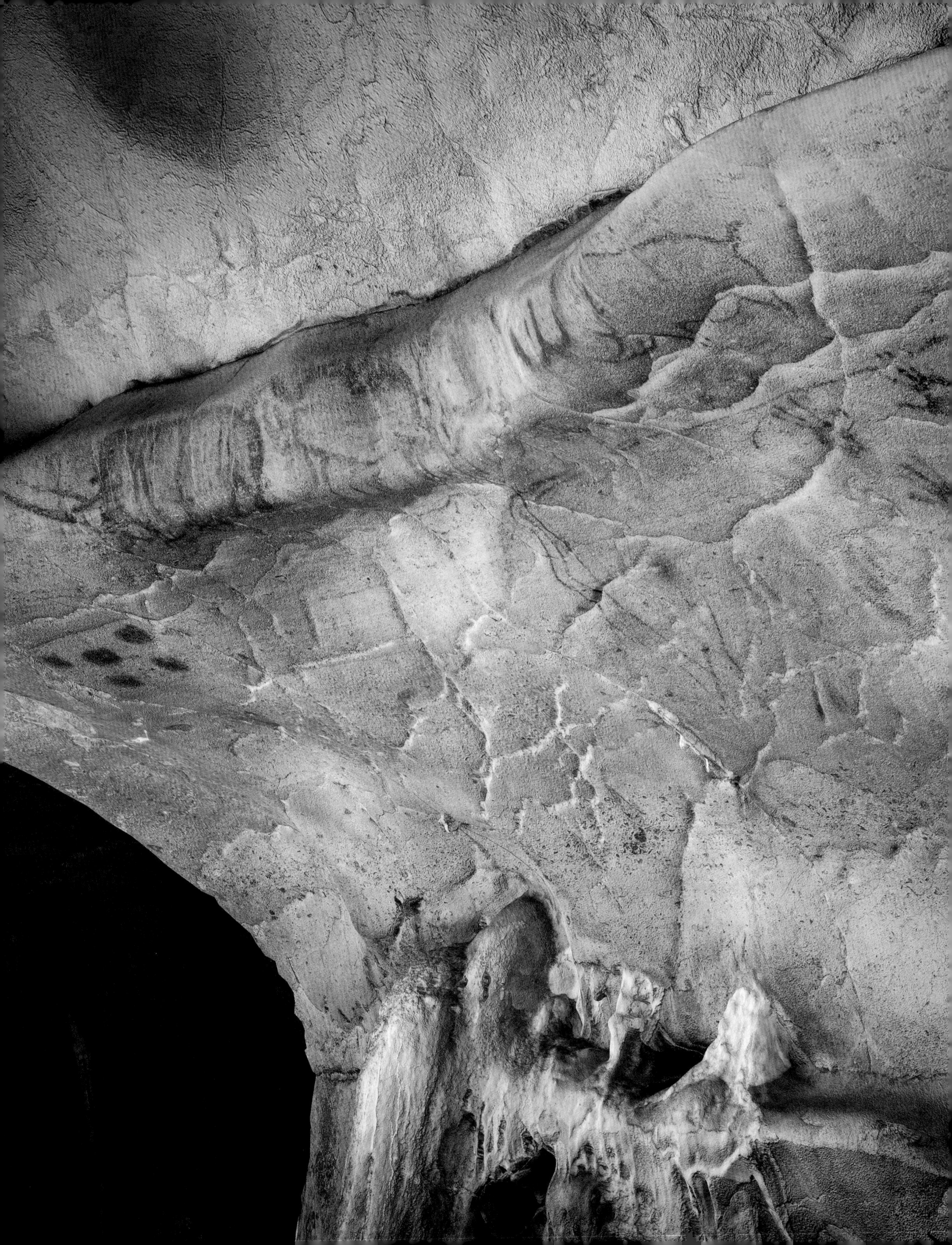

In total, twelve positive and negative hands are found in the cavity, belonging to a woman or an adolescent and a tall man. By covering their hands in ochre and placing them on the wall, as here on the Panel of Positive Hands, the artists of Chauvet-Pont d'Arc were certainly performing an act of great symbolic value, possibly related to a magical or supernatural belief. Were these actions connected to initiatory rites, to cults with a religious connotation? According to the hypothesis of parietal art created in a shamanic context proposed by Jean Clottes and his colleague David Lewis-Williams, placing one's hand covered in pigment on the rock may have corresponded for Palaeolithic humans to an attempt to communicate with forces present on the other side of the wall. Piles of rock were assembled at the foot of the panel by groups of humans who occupied the cavern. Are the painted figures symbolically related to this artificial arrangement? The hypothesis is plausible.

By placing his hand on the rock, did the artist wish to enter into contact with forces present on the other side of the wall?

To the right of the positive hands, dotted signs forming a semi-circle are associated with a feline's head, and a mammoth that seems to be turning its back to it.

(Exploration)

The Panel of Positive Hands and the Frieze of Rhinoceroses.

Above the Panel of Positive Hands, a frieze containing a procession of rhinoceroses entirely decorates a ledge. The first one has a huge horn and it seems to be heading towards the end of the chamber. A sign in the shape of a "W", specific to Chauvet-Pont d'Arc, faces the rhinoceros on the right.

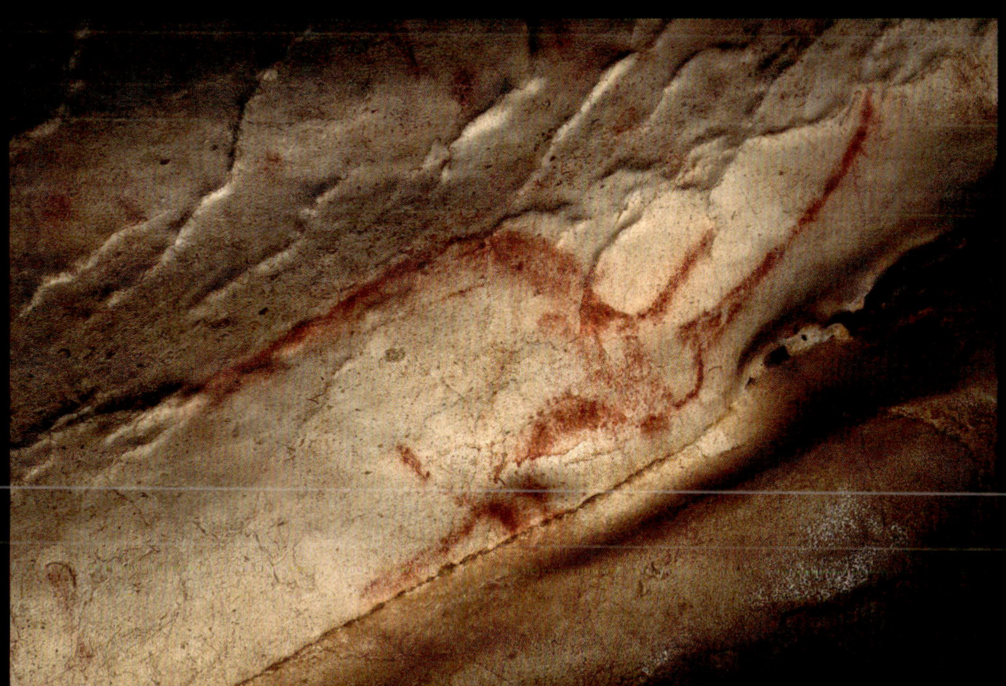

3D technology makes it possible to enhance the details of this little rhinoceros placed at the foot of the Panel of Positive Hands, which is difficult to see from the walkways barring access to the floors of the cave. We also see the smoothing of the wall due to passage of cave bears over thousands of years.

HILLAIRE CHAMBER

We come to this huge chamber through a narrow passage that opens up from the Red Panels Chamber, followed by a large space with almost no figures: the Candle Gallery. Once past this symbolic threshold closing off the first area of the cave, which is essentially decorated with red paintings, we enter a different pictorial universe, characterized by the presence of black pigment and engravings. When first stepping into the Hillaire Chamber, the eye is attracted to a large natural collapse, about a dozen metres in diameter, circumvented by the network of walkways. The vaults and walls form folds, outgrowths, and particularly marked recesses that must have aroused the artists' curiosity and stimulated their creativity. Several hanging rocks are in fact abundantly covered with engravings.

The Hillaire Chamber numbers nine groups of figures or decorated panels combining several dozen animals and signs, which make it one of the most artistically rich sections of the cavity. The Aurignacian creators used every technique here, with a marked predominance of finger tracing, charcoal drawing, stumping and engraving. On the north wall of the chamber, the triptych composed of the Panel of Horses, the Alcove of the Lions and the Panel of Cervids represents a highpoint in Palaeolithic parietal art, with a masterful assembly of horses, aurochs, reindeer, felines and rhinoceroses. The spectacular staging must have been intentional on the part of the artists: we see this monumental panel on the opposite wall as soon as we enter the Hillaire Chamber and we are irresistibly drawn to it. 36,000 years after their creation, these Aurignacian masterpieces go on casting their spell.

(Exploration)

The Panel of Horses.

(opposite)
This little white horse on the south wall of the Hillaire Chamber was executed using the finger tracing technique. The putty-like outer layer is removed with the fingers to expose the underlying white rock.

The Panel of the Engraved Horse, six metres long, comprises thirteen animals in all. In some places the lines cover cave bear scratches (the mammoth's hump on the right).

In this black charcoal drawing on a rock pendant, the technique of stump, or shading, was used to give this little cave bear volume, further emphasized by the rounded shape of the wall.

Horse engraved with the fingers on a hanging rock in the Hillaire Chamber, covering cave bear scratches.

(following pages)
View of the triptych formed by the Panel of Cervids, the Alcove of the Lions and the Panel of Horses on the north wall of the Hillaire Chamber. Total length: 10 metres.

The Panel of Horses alone (detail opposite and following pages) concentrates all the genius of the artist, or the small number of artists, of the Chauvet-Pont d'Arc cave. Their excellent draughtsmanship is visible in the outlines of these aurochs, shading lends them life and volume, and fine engraving skilfully silhouettes and emphasizes the shapes of the animals: twenty in all on a wall of less than four square metres. Heading the study of this panel, the prehistorians Carole Fritz and Gilles Tosello have demonstrated that after scraping the surface of the rock to prepare the support, the artists successively represented the rhinoceroses on the left, two confronted rhinoceroses and the aurochs, finishing their animal scene with four horses. The dorsal lines of the horses harmoniously cling to the movement of the wall. This highly realistic work continues to excite the admiration of prehistorians and visitors alike.

The Panel of Horses alone concentrates all the genius of the artist, or the small number of artists, of the Chauvet-Pont d'Arc cave.

(Interactive immersion)

The Panel of Horses and the Skull Chamber.

(opposite)
Detail of aurochs in the Panel of Horses, drawn in charcoal on a white background obtained by previously scraping the substrate. Shading and the natural relief of the wall are used to give volume to the figures.

(following pages)
View of the Panel of Horses and the side of the Alcove of the Lions. Above the charcoal drawing of aurochs, engravings antedating the main panel are visible. They were obliterated when preparing the rock substrate.

This is a unique case in Palaeolithic cave art: two woolly rhinoceroses (*Coelodonta antiquitatis*) represented during an aggressive confrontation, possibly two rival males during a mating dance, and a scene most likely first observed in nature.

Starting from the bottom of the panel in this detail of the Panel of Horses, we observe the use of engraved silhouetting to give shape to the first of these four horses. Note their extraordinarily expressive eyes.

On the left panel of the Alcove of the Lions, felines and horses are assembled, almost overlapping, in a complex composition. Does each species correspond to a symbol connected to other animals according to a coded structure whose meaning escapes us?

(above)
Masterfully executed, this horse in the Alcove of the Lions, with a body covered in orange resulting from a natural calcite flow, is one of the masterpieces of Chauvet-Pont d'Arc.

(opposite)
In the Alcove of the Lions, the artists have represented a mating scene between a male lion (below) that seems to be calling to a sitting female showing her fangs. Incontestably, the artists were remarkable observers of the world of nature of which they formed an integral part.

(following pages)
The bottom of the Alcove of the Lions, from which a horse and a bison seem to be escaping, almost in terror. Symbolic bowels of the earth or animal spirits born of a prehistoric shaman's vision?

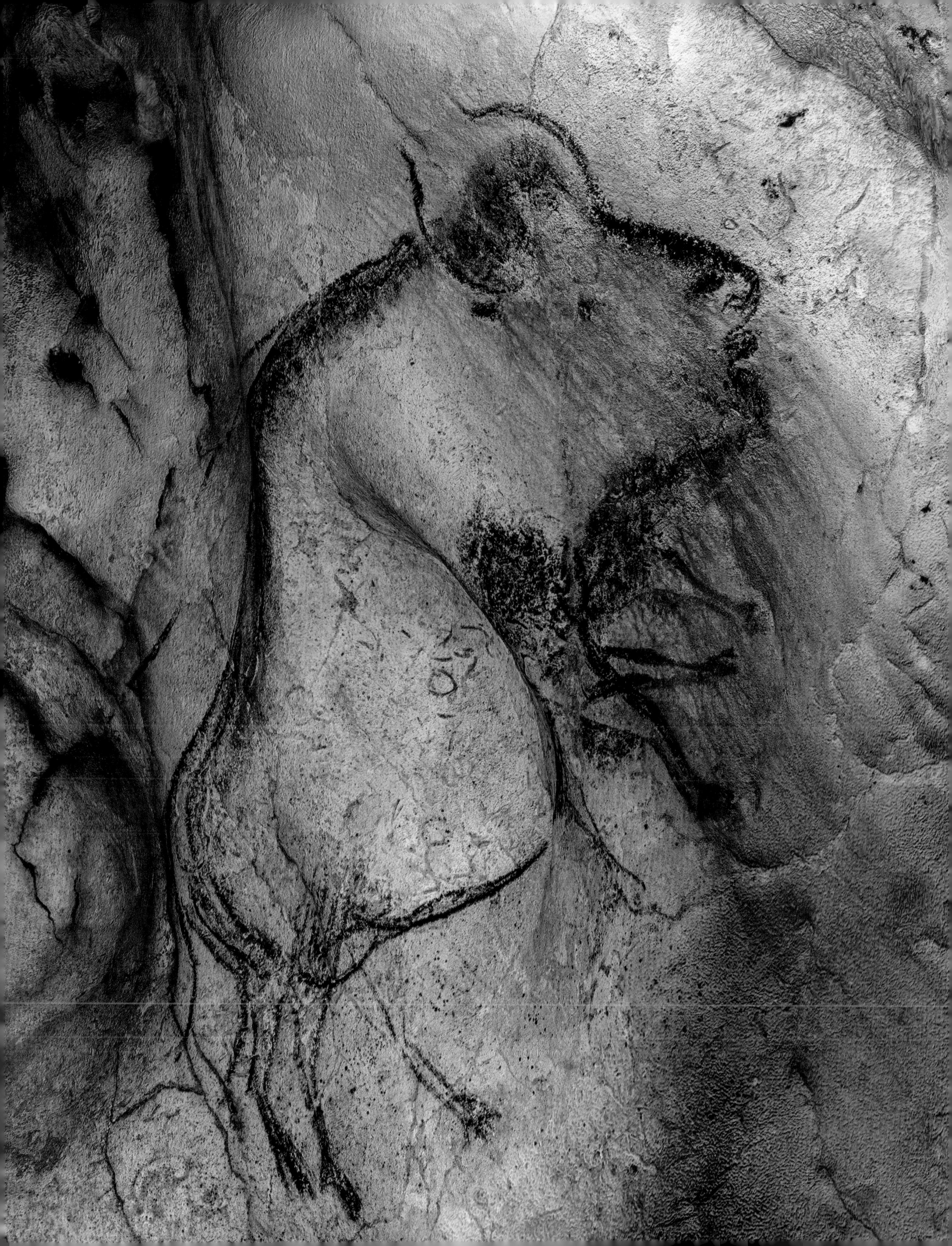

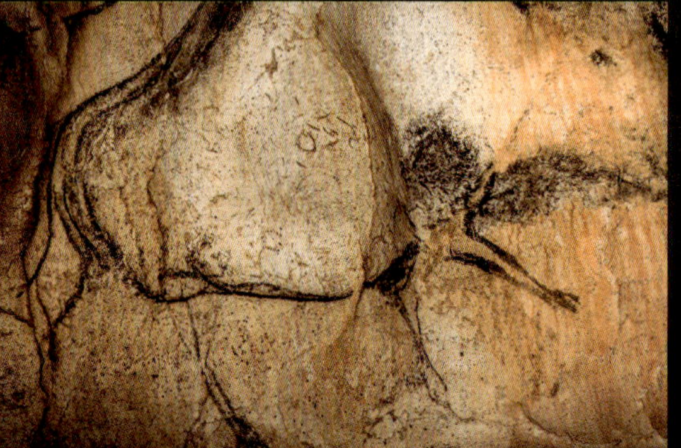

On the rough walls of the Ardèche cavity, the Aurignacian artists have left an unforgettable testimony to their many talents. For example, as Jean Clottes and Marc Azéma, assisted by the specialist in animal behaviour Craig Packer have shown, they were capable of representing veritable ethological scenes taken from previous observation of felines in the wild. They show knowledge of the male's mating behaviour, pre-mating behaviour between male and female, and the collective hunt. Once back in the darkness of the cavern, they not only executed these realistic paintings with consummate skill, but with their proficiency at representing movement, they gave life to their animal models approaching what existed in the real world. This is the case of the poignant bison in the Alcove of the Lions (opposite), galloping on the rock with its doubled legs, but also of at least one of the great cats in the End Chamber, represented with extended hindquarters. This wish to transpose on the walls the animation that signifies life itself, starting with Chauvet-Pont d'Arc 36,000 years ago, is a constant in Palaeolithic parietal art. In this vein, the prehistorian and scientific team member, Marc Azéma has shown that almost half the bestiary depicted in the French decorated caves was in fact animated. For this specialist, "*the animals depicted on the walls are not simply symbols devoid of life: they move, change and interact.*" And what if before our amazed eyes, in the dark of the Ardèche cavity, these were the first animated scenes, the beginnings of graphic narration and pre-cinema?

This bison of the Alcove of the Lions is represented galloping as shown by its skilfully doubled legs. One more proof of the immense talent of Palaeolithic artists capable of representing movement and with it, life.

(following pages)
The Panel of Cervids that follows the Alcove of the Lions counts thirteen animals and a red mark in its centre. The reindeers' antlers are curved forward, and those of the stags are more or less rectilinear.

(Animation)

The galloping bison in the Alcove of Lions.

Powerful and filled with vital energy, this woolly rhinoceros with a splendid curved horn (opposite) is a good illustration of the importance of 3D technology for transmitting the cave art of Chauvet-Pont d'Arc. When we move away from the triptych on the north wall in the Hillaire Chamber, heading toward the Megaloceros Gallery and beyond the magnificent End Chamber, this animal drawn in charcoal appears quite deformed when seen in an alcove far from the walkway in the actual cavity. However the 3D survey in 2010 makes it possible to observe it facing the wall, from the same viewpoint as the Aurignacian artists, and judge its true proportions. It is then that we perceive the Palaeolithic artists' capacity for observation and their judicious use of nature and the rock's contours in their drawing of the rhinoceros. We see an emblematic image of an art in the form of a hymn to the power of the animal world, omnipresent in the surroundings and the minds of men.

3D makes it possible to see from the same viewpoint as the Aurignacian artists, revealing the full extent of their talent.

(preceding pages)
The majestic triptych composed of the Panel of Horses, the Alcove of the Lions and the Panel of Cervids with the rhinoceros of the alcove in the foreground.

In total, 72 woolly rhinoceroses *(Coelodontha antiquitatis)* are depicted in Chauvet-Pont d'Arc, like this one in the alcove.

CHAMBER OF THE SKULL

Situated in the prolongation of the Hillaire Chamber, this chamber attracts our attention by the dozens of cave bear skeletal remains and skulls strewn on the ground, some of which seem to be immersed in a gangue of calcite. The feeling of mystery grows with the presence of a rock fallen from the vault in the middle of the chamber, on which one of the skulls has been placed. Here this theatricality, already employed in some of the decorated panels, becomes positively gripping. As noted by Carole Fritz and Gilles Tosello, the whole chamber resembles an amphitheatre with "stands" made of benches of gray clay that seem to encircle it. This idea is reinforced by other observations made by the speleo-archaeologist Yann-Pierre Montelle. Some of the natural benches seem to have been reworked by human hands. Moreover, the main block on which the skull was placed seems to have been intentionally arranged to fulfil this function, possibly one of a symbolic nature, by placing a second rock that seems to prop up and seal the first.

Such arrangements, if they are confirmed by future research, tend to suggest that the cavity was entirely organised by humans, as already partly shown by the team of geo-morphologists of the EDYTEM laboratory led by Jean-Jacques Delannoy. In the practice of a cult? Viewed from this perspective, the first rocks assembled in a pile in the preceding chambers, as well as the strange collapse in the Candle Chamber, may be construed as successive stages on a symbolic path converging on the symbolic core of the sanctuary. The Chamber of the Skull could then be seen as the first known theatre, placed under the sign of the bear—an animal feared and respected. Even to the extent of being considered as *"an intermediary between the world of the senses and the spirit world of which the cavern was the dwelling,"* according to the hypothesis of the anthropologist Joëlle Robert-Lamblin?

(opposite, and following pages)
The palaeo-zoologists leading the study of Chauvet-Pont d'Arc have counted 4000 skeletal remains of the species *Ursus spelaeus*, many of which are skulls of 200 individuals. A team of paleo-geneticists took samples of DNA from some of these remains, also dated with ^{14}C, indirectly confirming the age of the paintings of Chauvet-Pont d'Arc. The DNA analysis showed that the species *Ursus spelaeus*, physically present in the cavity and represented on its walls, disappeared circa 29,000 years ago.

MEGALOCEROS GALLERY

Close to the Panel of Cervids in the Hillaire Chamber, and just past the Alcove of the Rhinoceros, the Megaloceros Gallery is a sloping corridor leading to the inner sanctum of Chauvet-Pont d'Arc: the exquisite End Chamber. At the foot of the walls, one can see numerous vestiges of fires lit by men to burn the Scots pine used to obtain charcoal pigment. Ostensibly the black pigment used on the walls of the succeeding chamber was prepared here. More than ever, before these hearths and the tracings on the rock a few inches away, the Aurignacian presence is palpable and stirring for the visitor. The gallery takes its name from the large ice age mammals that adorn its walls, the impressive megaloceros (or giant deer) that could reach two metres at the withers, with huge antlers when mature. This animal certainly impressed the Aurignacians with its colossal size and height, so that it joined their sacred lexicon of animals in the final area of the sanctuary, the richest in masterpieces.

(preceding pages)
In the Chamber of the Skull, relatively devoid of parietal art, several reindeer are depicted on a hanging rock.

(opposite)
Above this megaloceros depicted at the entrance of the gallery, traces of older black paintings are visible, obliterated by the scraping that allowed the artists to prepare the substrate before drawing.

(following pages)
In the Megaloceros Gallery, the figuration of the spherically shaped hooves of this little woolly rhinoceros is seen in many other representatives of this same species at Chauvet-Pont d'Arc.

More than ever, the Aurignacian presence is palpable and stirring for the visitor.

In total, 52 horses *(Equus caballus*) are represented in the Chauvet-Pont d'Arc cave, or 11% of the bestiary. This one was traced in charcoal and stumped.

This pubic triangle, represented with the vulva, is one of seven found in the whole of the cavity. Wide engraved lines are used here.

Just before the end of the Megaloceros Gallery, this ibex with outsized horns drawn on the right wall seems to show the way to the End Chamber, with an invitation to attend the final display created by the Aurignacians.

As Dominique Baffier and Valérie Feruglio showed during their study of the parietal art of the Megaloceros Gallery, it is not a single rhinoceros represented in the painting opposite, but two. Above the main animal, a second one is depicted, reduced to a single dorsal line and two characteristic ears, known as "double arcs". We find this type of representation of the two ears on the central rhinoceros, which turns its back on the other one, following a stylistic convention. The ventral band of the animal also still puzzles scientists. Could it be the seasonal shedding of an animal with a thick coat or the concentration of the wool around the belly? What is remarkable is that this same way of representing rhinoceros ears is found in the Rumanian decorated cavity of Coliboaia, thousands of kilometres from Chauvet-Pont d'Arc, and also attributed to the Aurignacian period. This is proof, according to the prehistorian Jean Clottes, that groups of humans travelled long distances across Europe. Bringing with them, during their migrations, their founding myths and the animal images that illustrated them.

Rhinoceros in the Megaloceros Gallery.

END CHAMBER

And if, at Chauvet-Pont d'Arc, the arrangement of the panels, the succession of animal themes, the structuring of the underground space and the choice of colours from the entrance of the cave to its depths, as well as the slow artistic crescendo from one chamber and one wall to the next were in fact a sort of cleverly staged pathway designed to prepare for the final shock, the most amazing revelation? Once past the threshold marked by the end of the Megaloceros Gallery, arriving in an area where the excess of CO_2 can lead to a loss of bearings and lucidity, the monumental panels of the End Chamber with their multitude of striking images beckon to the visitor. On admirable golden-hued walls, felines, mammoths, rhinoceroses, bison and horses splash the cavity with their beauty, their force and their vitality. Welcome to the final recess of the cave-sanctuary where the Aurignacians created their most awe-inspiring masterpiece for eternity… Humanity's very first.

(Exploration)

The End Chamber.

•

(preceding pages)
The artist depicted vibrissas, the whiskers serving as sensory organs above the mouth, on these two lions found to the left of the End Chamber's monumental panel.

(above)
The End Chamber's monumental panel, twelve metres long, is organised around a central alcove in which a small horse has been drawn. To the left, the Panel of Rhinoceroses and to the right, the Panel of Lions.

(following pages)
Detail of the Panel of Rhinoceroses. In the background, the alcove of the small horse and the beginning of the Panel of Lions.

Before the discovery of Chauvet-Pont d'Arc, the rhinoceros was rarely seen in Palaeolithic parietal art. The Panel of Rhinoceroses alone features at least seventeen. These animals are represented in perspective (above), outlined with engraving.

On this rhinoceros hugging the contours of the wall, the artist used a white reserve between the two hindquarters, producing the distance that separates them from the observer's viewpoint, and emphasized the head and the horn with a white engraving traced in the black pigment.

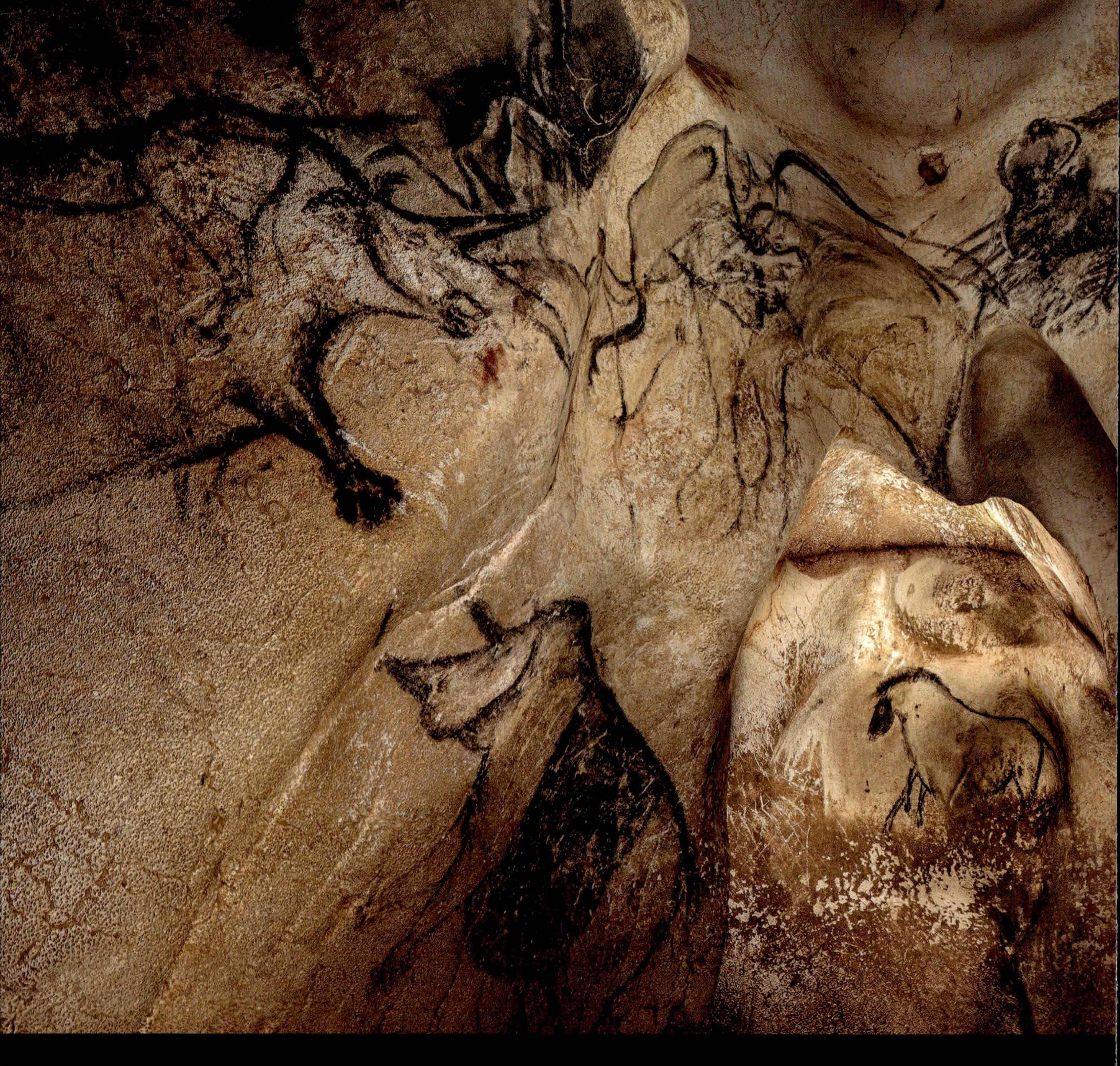

In the heart of the central alcove of the vast panel in the End Chamber, this little horse of barely 60 centimetres occupies a symbolically predominant place. We are baffled by this choice. Did this species play a major part in the myths or tales recounted by the iconography in the End Chamber? This is a possibility. Whatever the reason, the figure is full of life, with four short lines engraved in front of its nostrils, in all likelihood depicting its breath. Jean Clottes, the first director of the scientific study of Chauvet-Pont d'Arc also notes that the artists prepared the rock prior to executing the animal's image, as is the case in other places in the cavity. The wall has even been scraped to suggest the shape of the horse, including a suggestion of the head and an eye. "*The impression is one of an animal leaping from the depths of the rock,*" explains the specialist. On the upper right border of the niche, a bison produces a similar effect of leaping from the rock. Under the bison, two mammoths overlap into each other, according to Marc Azéma and Bernard Gély's description. A judicious balance of charcoal and clay expertly reproduce the main animal's gray coat.

The End Chamber's monumental panel is organised around this little horse in the alcove.

(opposite, and following pages)
3D technology makes it possible to light, reveal and enhance the small horse in the alcove of the vast panel in the End Chamber.

(Interactive immersion)

The End Chamber's monumental panel.

The sixteen felines in the Panel of Lions are all facing left, except one, seen to the left of the composition, facing another lion.

(following pages)
Detail of the Panel of Lions, showing a pride of cave lions, males and females, hunting bison. This species did not have a mane like today's lions.

With 80 individuals, the cave lion is the king of the bestiary of the Chauvet-Pont d'Arc cave. On the eponymous panel, sixteen felines are leaning towards a group of bison, to the left of the scene, which they seem to be on the point of attacking. A wide range of perfectly mastered techniques — drawing, stumping, silhouetting — were employed to arrive at this absolute masterpiece of Palaeolithic art. As shown by Craig Packer, animal behaviour specialist, the sex of some of the big cats can be identified, as well as their age, with at least five males, a female and five lion cubs. Movement has also been depicted through lining up the individuals and the extension of some of the hindquarters. According to the anthropologist Joëlle Robert-Lamblin, many of the feline muzzles may recall human profiles. Is it possible that the artists allegorically depicted *"man's symbolic double, hunters like them"* in the features of these agile, terrifying lions? This hypothesis, implying a notion of fluidity and porosity between species, widespread in shamanic or traditional societies, is backed up by the existence of half-man, half-lion statuettes from the same Aurignacian period (see pg. 35).

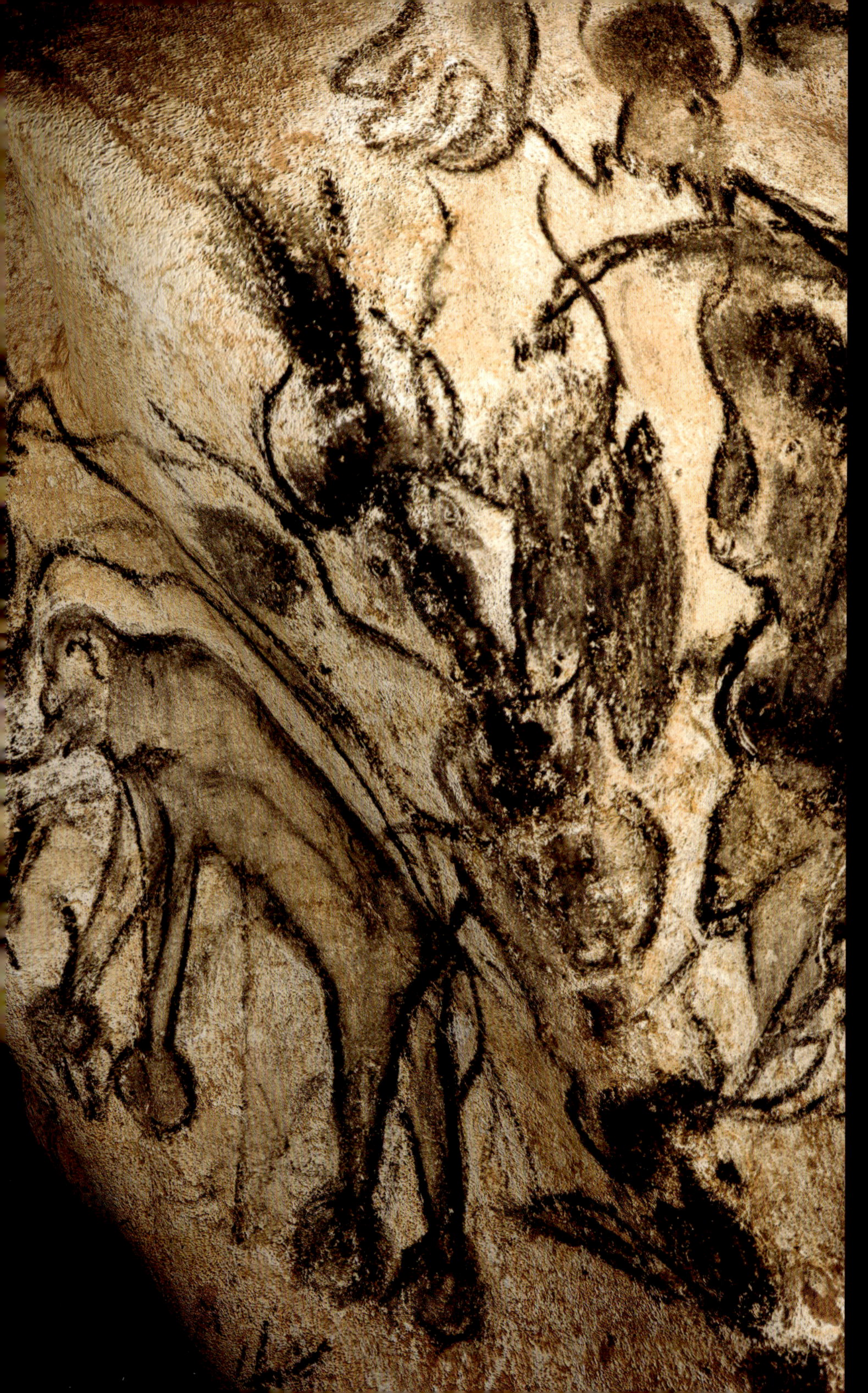

To the right of the monumental panel's central niche, four bison are represented, viewed from the front, on a natural ridge of the rock

Standing back from the Panel of Lions, this little rhinoceros seems to be observing the dynamic hunting scene happening before its eyes.

To the right of the monumental panel, this bison shown with its body in profile and its head viewed from the front, making astute use of the relief of the rock and its ridge, illustrates the artists' prowess in rendering both natural and animal volumes.

(following pages)
View of the hanging rock with a Venus. In the background the End Chamber's monumental panel.

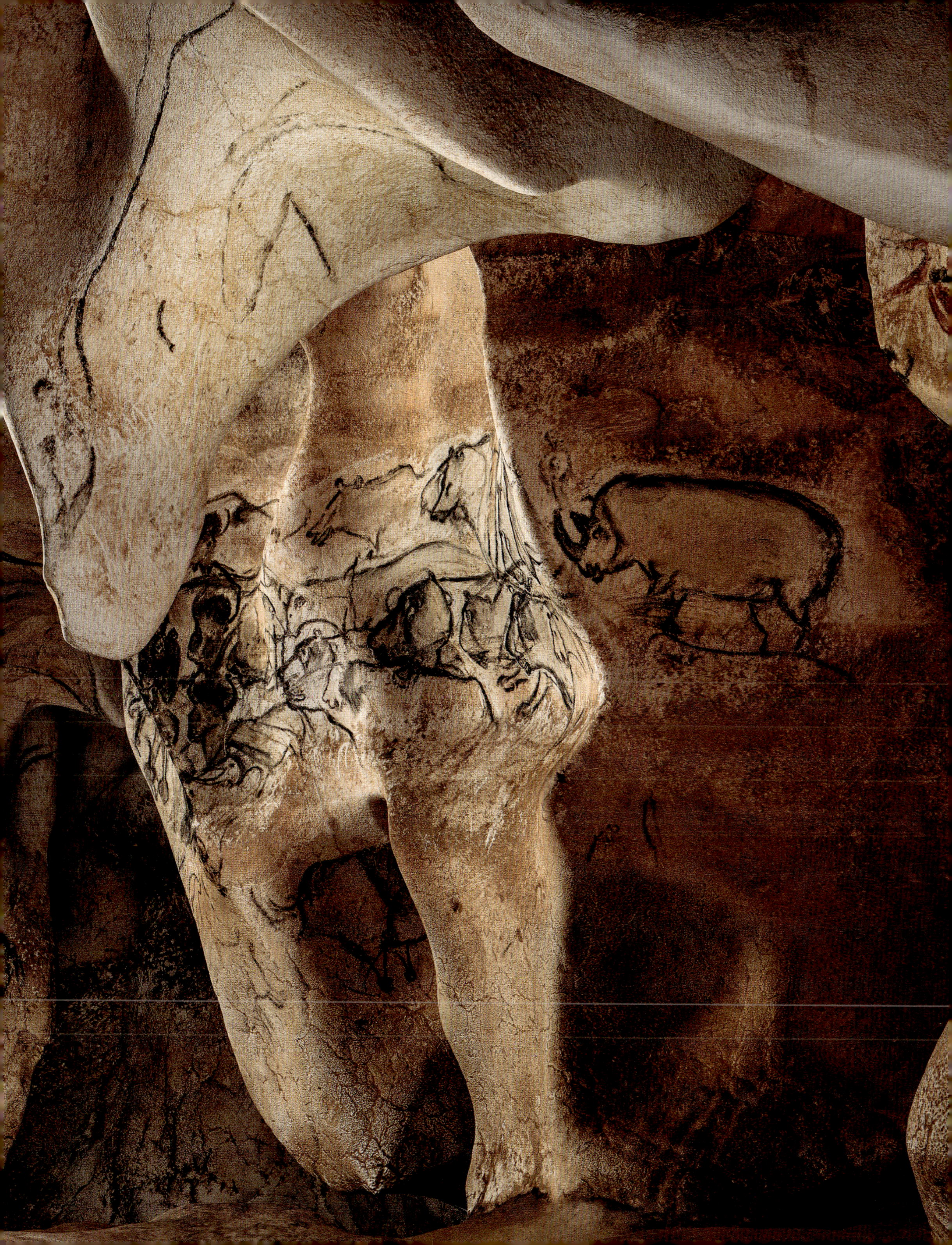

At the bottom of the End Chamber, to the right of the large composition, the Aurignacian artists created Chauvet-Pont d'Arc's most mystifying work, and its most disturbing symbol. Two female legs and a pubic triangle are traced in charcoal on a hanging rock, as though enlaced with the figure of a bison, its forequarters melding into one of the legs. The picture, with its impenetrable meaning, is completed by the figure of a feline overlooking the ensemble. What is the meaning of this prehistoric "Venus" that suggests and partly heralds the female statuettes of the Gravettian period, subsequent to the Aurignacian? Could this be a fertility symbol giving birth in the painters' imaginary to the fantastic bestiary surrounding it? Or a prehistoric shaman's vision of a half-woman, half-bison? Beyond all interpretations, none of which suffice to understand the complexity of the message inscribed on the walls, Chauvet-Pont d'Arc remains an enigma and a source of unanswered questions. These final images of the sanctuary before returning to daylight are images that haunt us still.

At the back of the Venus hanging rock, there are three successive planes featuring lions, a bison and a horse, which seem to appear from a crevice.

(following pages)
The last recesses of the End Chamber. The largest bison, to the right, has been dated with ^{14}C.

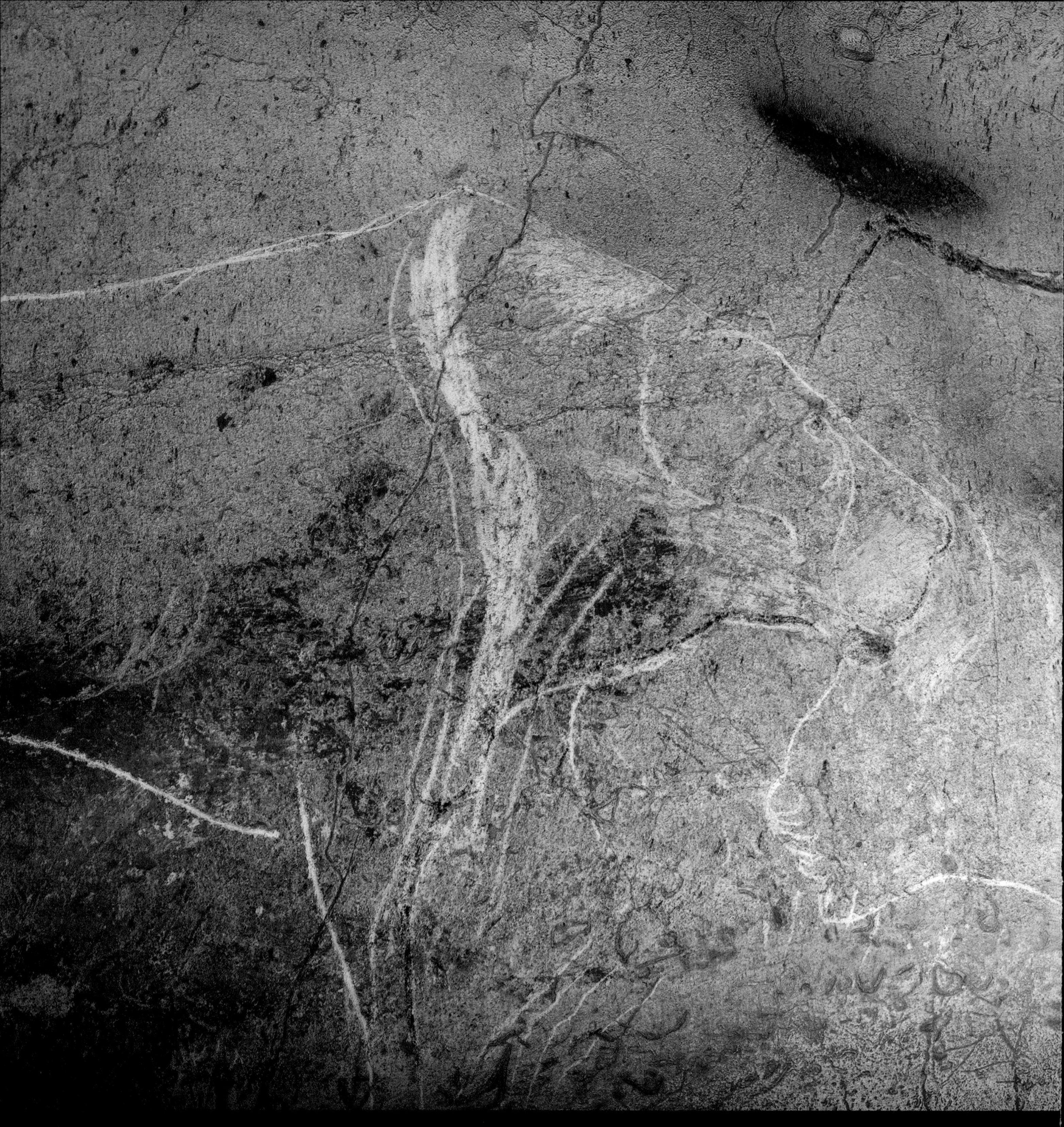

The time has come to quit the sanctuary, and leave the lions of the End Chamber in silence, along with all the other fantastic animals surrounding them.

Masterfully decorated 36,000 years ago, closed off 15,000 years later and rediscovered in 1994 by three speleologists, Chauvet-Pont d'Arc once again returns to its repose, far from the commotion of the world.

So as to share and offer it to humanity, whose common heritage it is, a reproduction of the art of the earliest times needed to be created in the mineralogical setting that gave birth to it.

On the right panel of the End Chamber, opposite the monumental panel, the artists represented two felines, one engraved and the other drawn, and the engraved head of a bison. Above and to the right: a pubic triangle drawn in black.

06

FROM THE CAVE
TO THE PONT-D'ARC CAVERN

The replica: an ambitious gamble

The Pont-d'Arc Cavern is the name given to the reproduction of Chauvet-Pont d'Arc, and its ambition is to transmit the emotion evoked by the paintings, the complex volumes of the cavity and all its mineralogical beauty. A world premiere that calls upon the most advanced technologies and the sensitivity of painters, plastic artists and sculptors.

In the years following the discovery of the Chauvet-Pont d'Arc cave and the decision to prohibit public access to protect its treasures, the idea of a replica surfaced — a replica capable of sharing this magnificent art of the earliest times with the public. After a first aborted attempt, in 2007 Pascal Terrasse, the president of the General Council of the Ardèche revitalized the ambitious project in conjunction with the Rhône-Alpes region and its president, Jean-Jack Queyranne. Razal, in the heights of Vallon-Pont d'Arc, two kilometres from the original cave, was chosen for its site. Once the studies and the architectural projects were completed in October 2012, the French minister of Culture Aurélie Filippetti placed the symbolic "first hand" on the Reproduction Space. She broke the ground for this unprecedented project ending in 2015 with the opening of the Pont-d'Arc Cavern, the name chosen for the replica.

In addition to the majority of the paintings, drawings and engravings, the project's ambition was also to reproduce the main geological and archaeological elements: mineral concretions, skeletal remains, hearths and imprints. The idea was to create a complete cave where all the characteristics of the underground milieu could be experienced: coolness, humidity and darkness. A cave capable of stirring the same emotion as Chauvet-Pont d'Arc, while remaining scientifically exact. The Pont-d'Arc Cavern is thus the first of its kind in the world. Never before has a decorated cavity of such size been copied with its floors, its decorated walls, its vaults and its archaeological, paleontological and mineralogical wealth.

Prior to the start of construction at Razal, this ambitious project necessitated thousands of hours of study, drawing and programme design. Starting in 2009, the creators of the 3D model completed the first stage in conjunction with scenographers and scientists. It was a question of selecting the most interesting and spectacular parts of the Chauvet-Pont d'Arc cave from a mineralogical, paleontological and artistic viewpoint. The result of this work, known as anamorphosis, is a precise plan in three dimensions of a new cavity comprising a surface area of 3,000 square metres whereas the original measures 8,500 square metres. Anamorphosis retains the succession of main chambers including the decorated zones and folds the original cave to increase surface area. Together the walls, floors and vaults of the Cavern represent a total area of 8,180 square metres.

Once the plans were drawn up, this complex creation halfway between the reality of the original and an artificial copy had to be built within the context of the Reconstruction Space. To accomplish this prodigious task, more than 500 people employed by 35 companies went to work on this unprecedented project which conjugated technological

(Animation)

Principle of Anamorphosis of the Pont-d'Arc Cavern.

Reproduction of the ochre dots in the Brunel Chamber for the Pont-d'Arc Cavern, by the *Arc et Os* atelier in Montignac, Dordogne.

(following pages)
Data obtained from the Chauvet-Pont d'Arc 3D model made it possible to design the anamorphosis of the replica. The Pont-d'Arc Cavern is supported from the ground and suspended from the ceiling by means of a network of metallic structures inside the building that contains it.

exploits, knowhow and industrial methods, painstaking skill and artistic sensitivity: 200 persons and 10 companies inside the Cavern alone.

◆

For nearly three years, a veritable jigsaw puzzle was built all over France, thousands of pieces of which (decorated panels, limestone concretions and skeletal remains) converged on the Razal site to take their place in the recreated cave. The conception of the Cavern represents a huge technological challenge in itself. Housed in an immense concrete shell, it was not built from the ground as one might imagine but suspended from the roof! The reason for this choice is the vast span of its vaults, i.e., the distance separating the various points of support could not ensure sufficient stability if the structure was built from the ground up. In order to accomplish this architectural and technological feat, an original process relying heavily on 3D recording data had to be invented.

The first stage of construction was the twisting of thousands of metal rods controlled by digital coordinates based on the 3D model. Once bent into the desired shape, these rods were welded together to obtain the first volumes of the cavity, vaults and walls. These took the shape of metal cages fixed to the ceiling of the concrete shell.

Welding and assembly of the metallic cages reproducing the volumes of the original cave at the Pont-d'Arc Cavern.

The 3D study made in the original cave is used to bend the metallic rods that give volume to the Cavern (above), before a wire mesh is fixed on the surface of each cage (above and right). The cages are then hung from the roof of the building (opposite).

To obtain the first rendering of the volume of the walls and vaults, mortar is projected on the wire-mesh metal cages. The mortar is then sculpted to arrive at more precise volumes, including the rock's crevices and reliefs.

Little by little, a rudimentary Cavern began to take shape, from the vaults to the base of the walls. The workers projected two coats of stone-coloured mortar on these cages, lending them a rocklike appearance. Then, trowel and stylus in hand, the sculptors took over to hone the volumes, dig crevices and interstices in the "rock", or make a contour or a bump stand out. This patient sculpting gave the wall its definitive volume, which was constantly checked against photographs taken in the original cave.

Sticking Close to Geological Structure

Once the volumes were copied in this way, it was the painters' turn to play their part and bring the final touches to the ersatz rock. These experts applied brown, red, black, yellow and clay tones with their brushes, sponges and a multicolour palette of ochre washes, earth colours and manganese. Little by little the Pont-d'Arc Cavern began to look exactly like the original. To stick as closely as possible to the geological structure, the sculptors and painters also had a precious tool called a *"carnet de faciès"* or "facies notebook" at their disposal. This is a veritable mineralogical alphabet composed of sixty profiles of walls and floors, created at Chauvet-Pont d'Arc by the geomorphologists from the EDYTEM laboratory, comprising colours of the walls and the soils, textures, materials, the hardness of each rock. This tool was put at the disposal of the plastic artists, painters and sculptors responsible for the reproduction of the decorated walls and limestone concretions.

Above, the Cavern's decorators bring the final touch to the reproduction of the walls and vaults. Each relief is compared to the data obtained from the 3D study of the original cave.

(following pages)
For a reproduction faithful to the original cavity, the ceiling of the Pont-d'Arc Cavern is decorated and given a patina.

While the Cavern was taking final shape on the heights of Vallon-Pont-d'Arc, the other pieces of the giant puzzle were being produced hundreds of miles from there. The twenty-seven decorated panels were reproduced in two ateliers in France. One is located in the town of Montignac, in the Dordogne, and the other in the city of Toulouse. In Montignac, a team of nine people first reproduced the meandering volumes of the walls before decorating them with paintings and drawings. First stage in the process: the moulding of a rudimentary shape carved in polystyrene blocks by a computer-aided five-axis robot, guided by data from the 3D model. Then the plastic artists applied medium on the resin wall, in the form of different types of mortar and cement to imitate the volumes with even greater precision. There again, the patient modelling was backed up by the projection of 3D images. These helped the sculptors find their position on the resin reproduction, guiding their hands to dig a furrow here, accentuate a crevice there, or build up a bump on the wall, which would later form a bison's back. In this way, gesture after gesture, all the complexity of the mineral substratum was brought to life in the studious ambience of the ateliers. This three-dimensional substratum was absolutely indispensable to the success of the copy, for the art of the Aurignacians was executed with great mastery on mineral canvases with complex shapes that fully participate in the final artistic project.

Exactitude for the Decorated Volumes

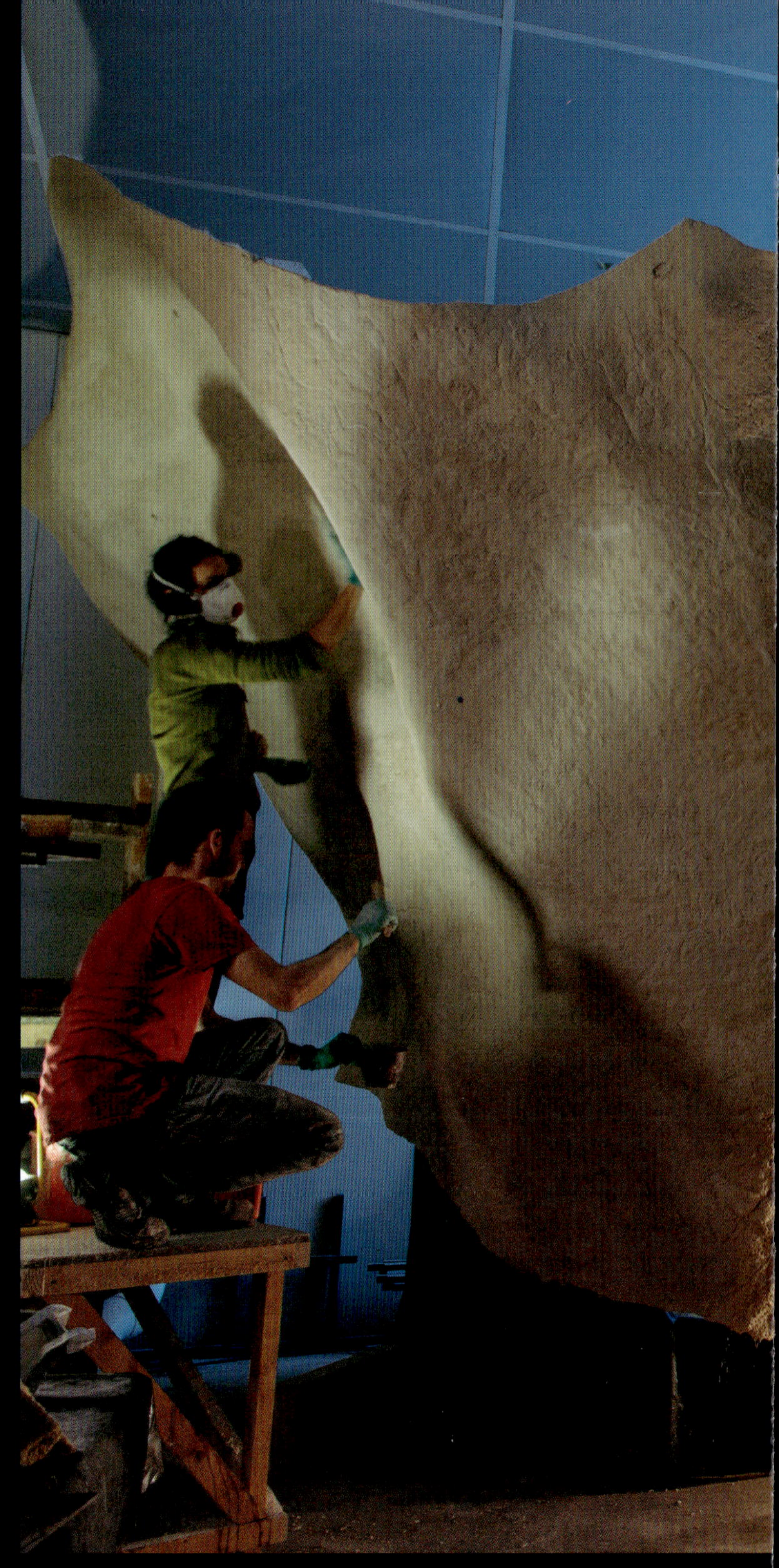

At the *Arc et Os atelier* in Montignac, Dordogne, the sculptors copy the volumes of the Panel of Lions in the End Chamber to the millimetre.

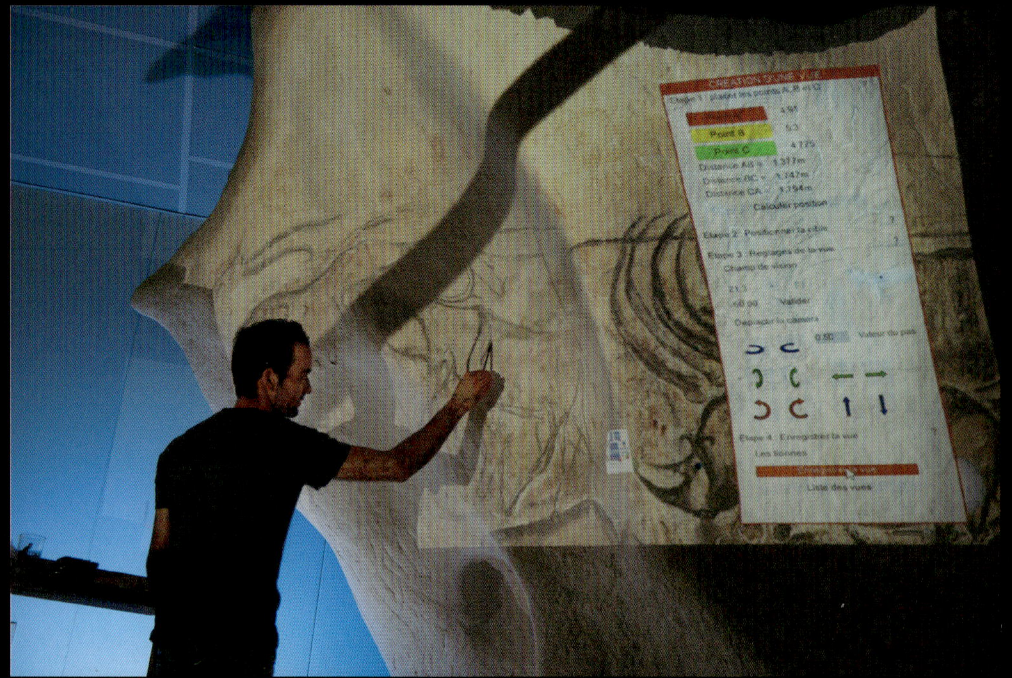

To reproduce the volumes of the Panel of the Rhinoceroses, the sculptors project the images from the 3D study of the original onto the resin wall, checking in this way the exactitude of their work.

A small plastic screen called "sesame" allows the artist to visualize the sculpted volume.

In his atelier in Montignac, Alain Dalis reproduces the lines of the engraved horse using the same finger tracing technique as the Aurignacians.

Once the volumes were a faithful reproduction of the original, the sculptors applied the final hues to the walls, basing their work on the range of shades established by the scientists. This palette includes umber and sienna, red and yellow ochres, black and more exceptionally, white. The superposition of coloured washes, applied with a brush or natural sponge, makes it possible to obtain deep, luminous hues and patinas, recalling the brilliance of the walls of Chauvet-Pont d'Arc. To stick even closer to the original, the copyists pushed the attention to detail even further and reproduced the shape of seashells incrusted in the rock.

The wall was at last ready for its final ornamentation in the form of paintings, drawings and engravings. This phase was accomplished partly in Montignac, but also in Toulouse where the two most spectacular compositions were prepared: the Panel of Horses and the Panel of Lions Hunting Bison.

In the Dordogne, powdered pigments and metal oxides were carefully prepared before their application to the walls with brushes and sponges. In order to copy some of the figures, Alain Dalis, specialist in prehistoric replicas, reproduced the creative gesture and its vital energy. Passing his fingers in the soft support, he defined the contours of the little engraved horse in the Hillaire Chamber, just as the Aurignacians did.

To reproduce the volumes of the decorated panels, the sculptors add medium to a resin wall, checking their work against the projected images from the 3D model.

To obtain the same brilliance as the original wall, the sculptor projects crushed calcite on the reproduction wall.

Aurignacian drawings are copied with pigments approaching those used in the originals. Here charcoal is used to draw a reindeer on the wall.

The responsibility weighing on the artistic teams was so great that they performed every gesture with the greatest concentration. Everyone felt that what they were transmitting was an important part of human history and culture. To make their effort successful, the artists were allowed access to the original cave for precious working sessions. An impelling and privileged immersion for these women and men of the 21st century, placed for a few hours before the Aurignacian masterpieces, which they were able to imbue so as to interpret and render them with the greatest possible accuracy.

Two Masterpieces Reproduced to Perfection

The two main masterpieces of Chauvet-Pont d'Arc were reproduced in Toulouse: the Panel of Horses and the monumental composition of the End Chamber, with its wealth of felines, rhinoceroses and bison. A delicate, complex task that led Gilles Tosello, both artist and member of the scientific team, to immerse himself in the gestures of his distant predecessors in order to reproduce them with the greatest precision. Who better than this specialist of parietal art, engrossed since 1998 in the volumes and images of the Ardèche cave, could copy these most beautiful of artistic gems with such success? In order to do so, Gilles Tosello used the same pigments as the authors of the originals. He did not hesitate to make his own charcoal crayons from burnt Scots pine, as did the draughtsmen of Chauvet-Pont d'Arc. He then imitated the rapid, precise gestures that breathed life into the lions and bison that seem to leap and gallop on the walls. He also made use of the innumerable scientific surveys and photographs taken from many different angles during various underground missions.

The result of this patient work is now visible in the Cavern. We may perceive the prodigious talent of the Aurignacian creators, the complexity of their artistic project, and the depth of the humanity they display there.

Some pigments used to reproduce the ochre coloration of the original wall are applied with a sponge, as seen on this hanging rock.

(following pages)
The skeletal remains and skulls of bears strewn on the floors of the original cave have been faithfully reproduced for the Cavern.

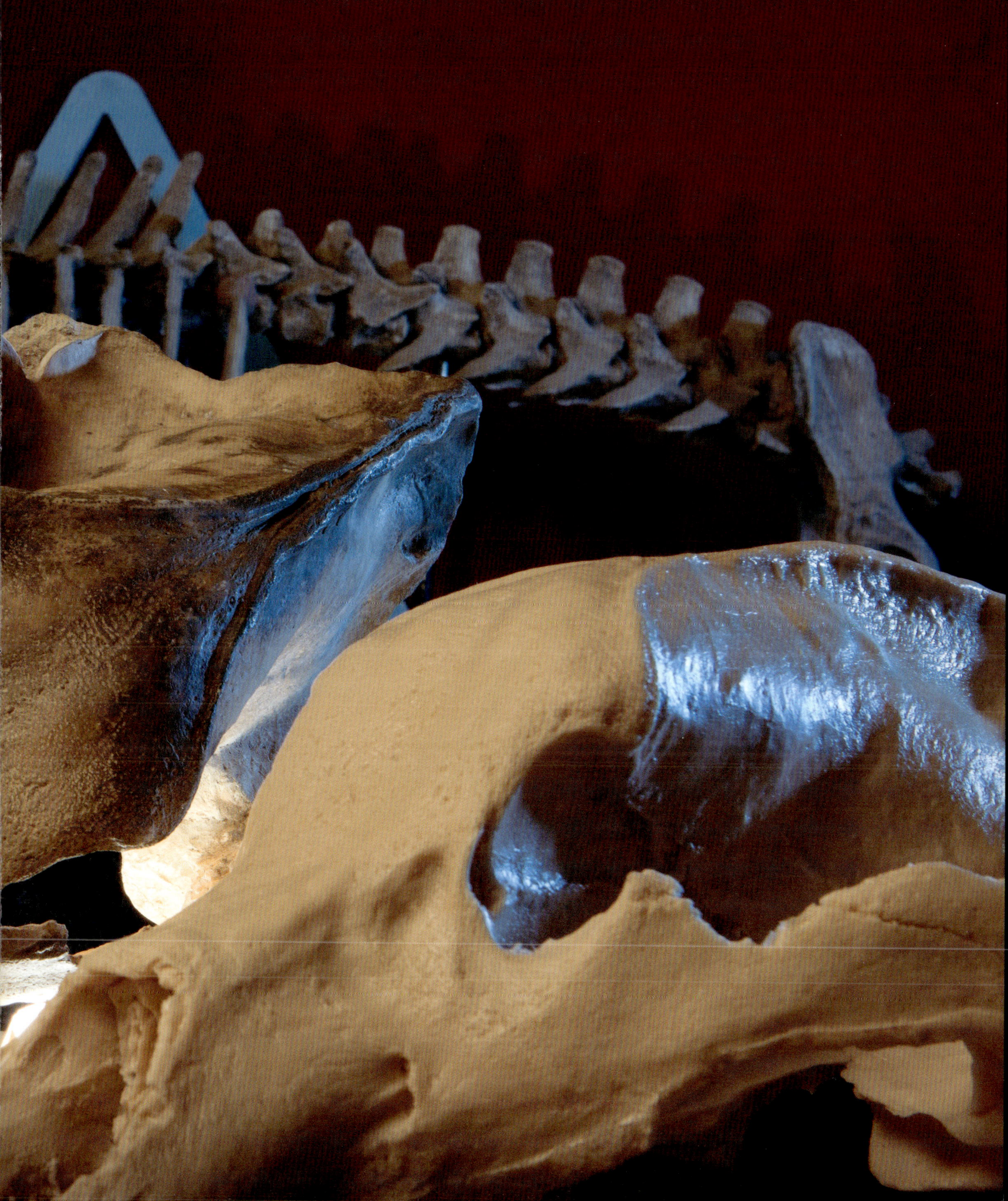

The copy of the countless speleothems, those limestone concretions that contribute to the scintillating magic of Chauvet-Pont d'Arc, was another indispensable element for the success of the Cavern. Made of calcite crystals formed by the subsurface flow of water, they take on very different forms. Draperies, stalagmites, stalactites, gours, pendants and fistulous concretions: all these mineralogical treasures were reproduced in Paris ateliers before converging at the Cavern. For this, Danièle Allemand and her team of moulders, sculptors and painters first researched and identified colours, textures and materials, a process that culminated in a veritable plastic alphabet. This preliminary phase also led the plastic artists to make mouldings in the undecorated parts of the cavity, allowing them to obtain textures and materials approaching those of the Chauvet-Pont d'Arc cave, whose floors and walls they were forbidden to touch. Then they sculpted, decorated and painted the concretions to arrive at shapes, colours and transparencies closest to the original. This meticulous work was lent additional precision from observations made in Chauvet-Pont d'Arc, and the precious information provided by the geomorphologists of the EDYTEM Laboratory at the University of Savoy (France). Finally, in the suburbs of Lyon, another team of plastic artists copied and aged numerous skeletal remains and the skulls of cave bears that litter the ground of the replica, based on casts of contemporary bears and photographs taken in the original cavity. More than one thousand skeletal vestiges were reproduced in this way.

(above)
Phénomènes **atelier sculptors study the mineral forms in the Chauvet-Pont d'Arc cave to achieve accuracy in their reproduction.**

Returning to the Cavern, the same specialists fine-tune the copy of the mineral concretions. Here a small red mammoth has been painted on top of large rock located close to the entrance.

(opposite)
Integration of the replica of the Panel of Horses, made in Toulouse, in the Pont-d'Arc Cavern

When entering the Cavern today, we plunge not only into the time of humans but into the time of the earth, when the Aurignacians lived and when geological events fashioned the underground world. Once past the airlock, all our senses are stimulated. The difference in temperature maintained with the outside produces a sensation of coolness and humidity. The smell of the underground milieu is suggested and the semi-darkness is conducive to contemplation. From the first steps taken along the perfectly reproduced floors, and facing the mineral draperies, we feel the same sense of wonder as at Chauvet-Pont d'Arc. This feeling deepens with the appearance of the first works of cave art, from the Panel of the Sacred Heart to the rhinoceros of the red frieze, then before the spectacular horses, reindeer and big cats of the Hillaire Chamber, or the impressive composition of the End Chamber, set off by the intriguing Venus of the hanging rock. Without a doubt, the Cavern is the faithful, poignant reflection of the parietal works of the Aurignacians encased in their geological context. This masterful creation finally makes it possible, and for many decades to come, to share the first masterpiece of humankind, and pay it the homage it so richly deserves.

◆

Gilles Tosello, artist and scientific team member, created a replica of this rhinoceros tucked in an alcove of the Hillaire Chamber for the Pont-d'Arc Cavern.

THE MAJOR ACTORS OF THE CAVERN

On the basis of the anamorphosis plan initially imagined by *Créatime* and carried out in 3D by *Perazio Engineering* in conjunction with the scenographers of the company *Scène* and the scientific team, *Campenon Bernard Régions* perfected the original construction process of reproduction, carried out by *Freyssinet-Cofex-AAB. The Socra-Campenon Bernard Régions* consortium directed the construction of the whole Cavern.

Phénomènes reproduced the speleothems and *Cossima Productions-Dasplet* the skeletal vestiges. *Arc et Os, Création Graphique* and *Déco Diffusion* copied the decorated panels.

The scientific committee headed by Jean Clottes approved the reproduction as a whole. Within the committee, the routine monitoring of the work of creation was ensured operationally by Jean-Michel Geneste, head of the scientific team, and Jean-Jacques Delannoy, in charge of the geomorphological study of the original, assisted by Philippe Fosse for subjects related to palaeontology.

Designed by the architects *Fabre-Speller* and *Atelier 3A*, the reproduction space includes five buildings that fit perfectly into the Ardèche landscape, including the one containing the Pont-d'Arc Cavern.

The structure housing the Pont-d'Arc Cavern was built in the heights of Vallon-Pont d'Arc, on the Razal site.

When entering the Cavern today, we plunge not only into the time of humans but into

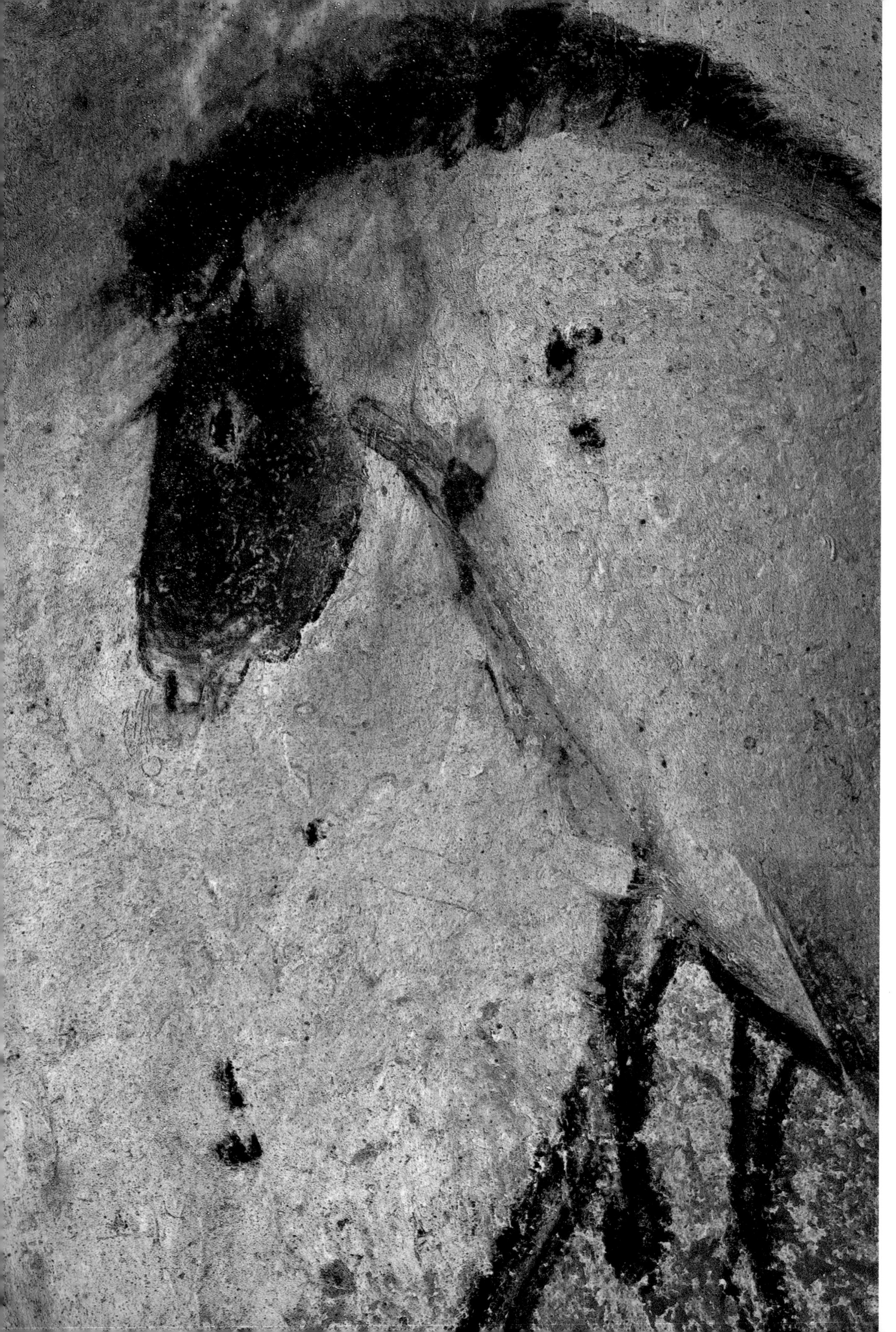

CONCLUSION

The Breath of the Human Spirit

In the month of June 2014, the UNESCO World Heritage Committee officially added the Chauvet-Pont d'Arc cave to the Shared Heritage of Humanity list.

Nearly twenty years after it was revealed to the world, this classification at last shows proper recognition of the parietal works it contains, a legacy of masterful creations from the first artists known to humanity. Among so many other examples attesting to this is the touching little horse in the alcove of the End Chamber accompanying these words, and the four delicate lines engraved in front of its nostrils, doubtless imitating the breath of life.

This recognition is even more amply deserved since this magnificent cave not only contains the earliest drawings, paintings and engravings to reach us; it precipitates all of humanity into a new era: composed of myths, questionings, knowledge and symbols.

For that matter, what did we know of our species, *Homo sapiens*, before the accomplished advent of the art and symbolism inscribed on the walls of the Ardèche cavity? To varying degrees our direct ancestors and other species *(Homo neandertalensis, Homo habilis, Homo erectus...)* left important traces of manual, cognitive, intellectual, and symbolic skills: worked stone tools, remains of fires, seashell necklaces, ochre blocks, graves.

But at Chauvet-Pont d'Arc, everything speeds up. In the form of animal figures, it is the sum of their capacity for investigation, interpretation and conceptualisation of the world that the Aurignacians reveal. Long before depicting them with a masterly hand on the walls, didn't they spend long hours spying on the mammals they picked for their sacred animal lexicon? Analysed their behaviour, understood the complex interactions between individuals and studied their anatomy with precision? Don't the attentive eyes of these women and men, associated with so much Aurignacian knowledge brought to light by archaeology, point to the starting point of a relationship to the world based on curiosity and questioning, a driving force that still defines us and motivates us on a daily basis? Add to that the insatiable desire to explore new territories that led the Aurignacians up the Ardèche River 36,000 years ago after exploring all of Eurasia. Isn't this the same desire that took *Homo sapiens* over the whole planet in the course of long, perilous migrations? And much later, wresting himself from the earth, to explore space?

And the founding myths, in all probability projected on the walls of Chauvet-Pont d'Arc in the shape of animal herds, bears leaping from the cracks in the rock, or female legs joined with bison; aren't they at the origin of those myths that still nourish our oral traditions, our texts and our unconscious?

Yes, Chauvet-Pont d'Arc may well constitute one of the spatial and temporal origins, already an achievement, of the human adventure. The Aurignacians inscribed a coded, elaborate work here and its lost meaning fascinates and baffles us still. A masterful work where each painted line, each incision in the wall, each stroke of charcoal applied to the mineral support, exudes the infinite complexity, depth and reality of the human being, in all his dimensions.

Pedro Lima scientific journalist
With **Benjamin Sadier**
PhD in geomorphology, scientific team member of the Chauvet-Pont d'Arc cave

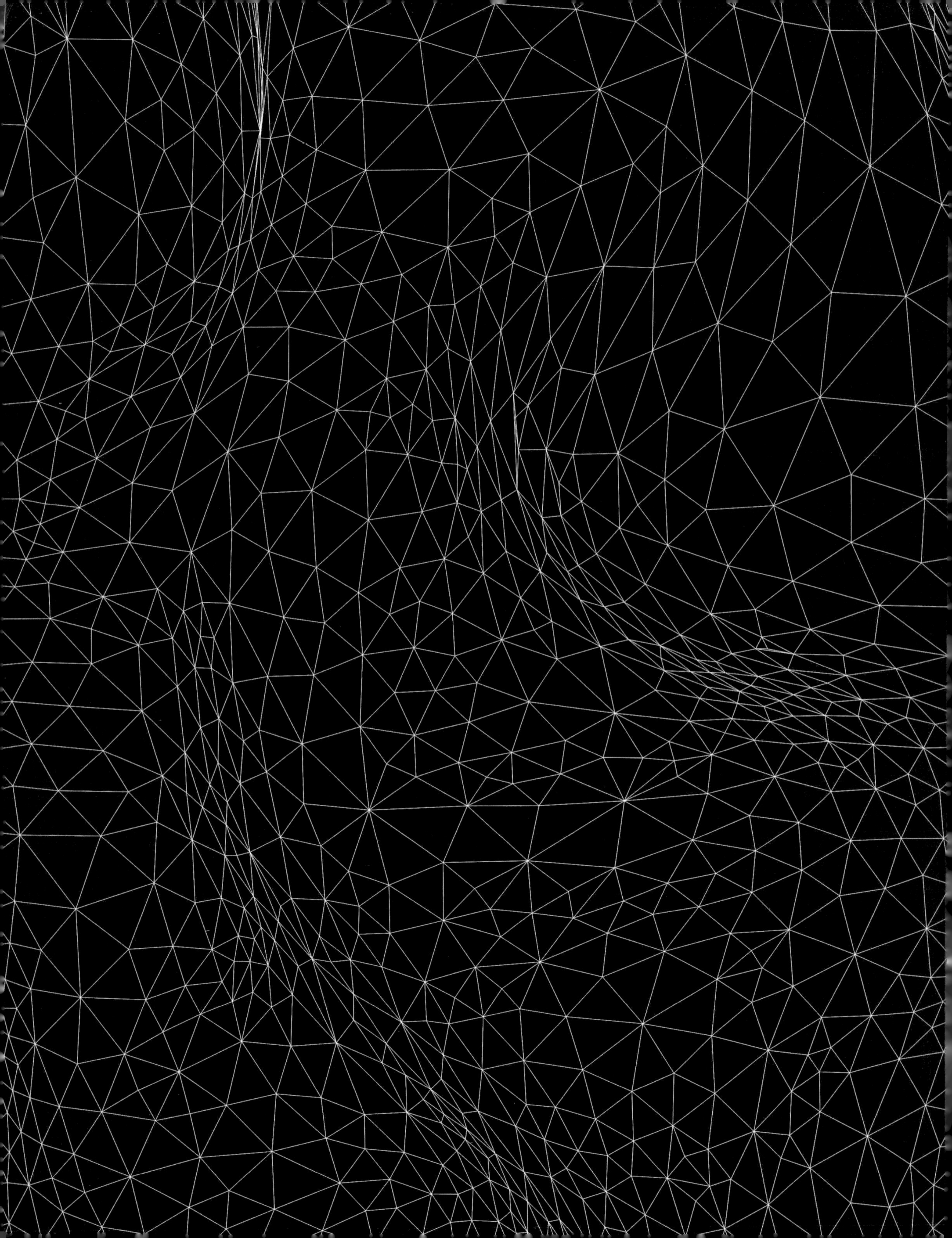

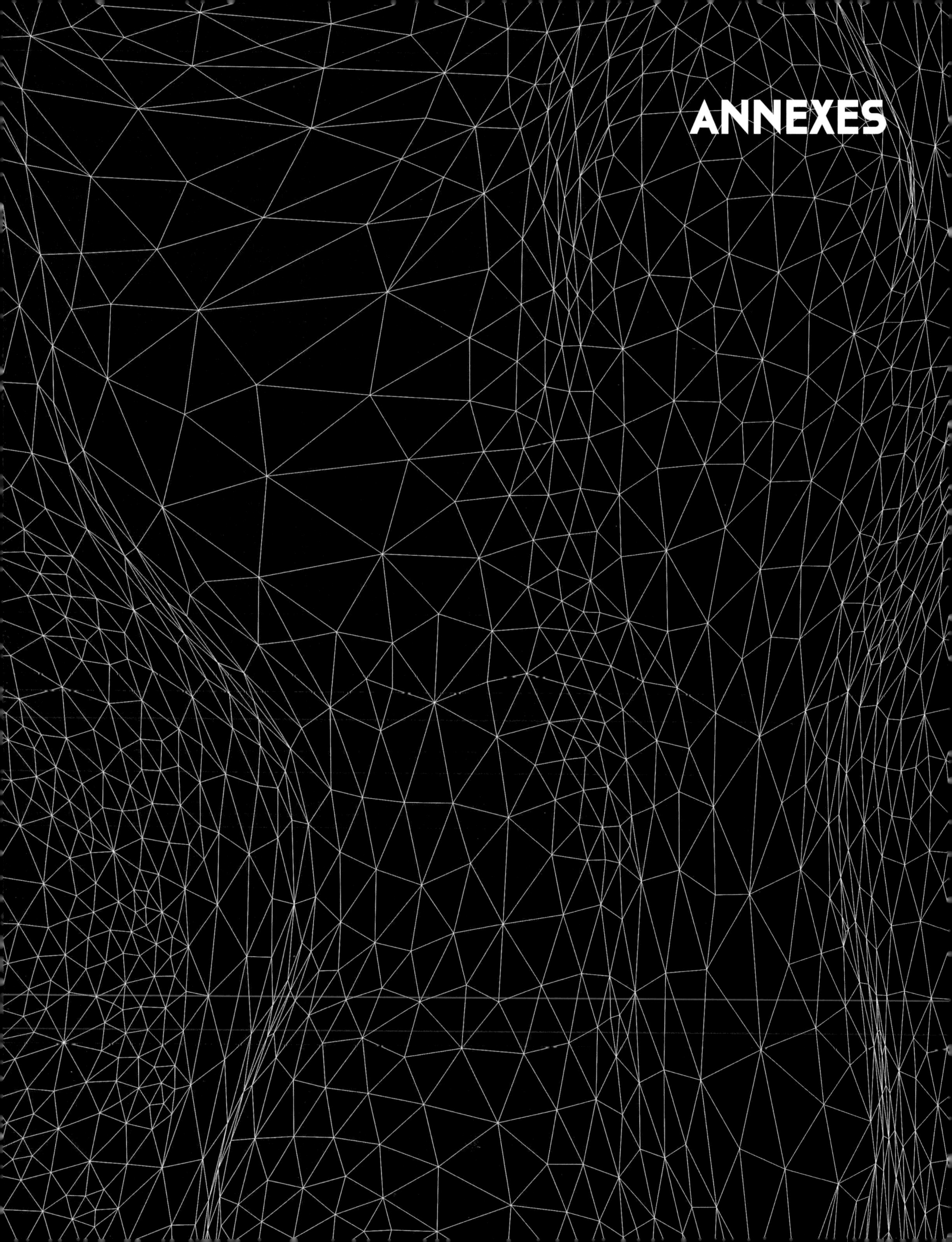

ANNEXES

ARDÈCHE
MONTÉLIMAR
DRÔME
VALLON-PONT-D'ARC
BOURG-SAINT-ANDÉOL
Natural Reserve of the Ardèche Gorges
SAINT-MARCEL-D'ARDÈCHE
PONT-SAINT-ESPRIT
GARD
VAUCLUSE

Underground and Prehistoric Sites in the Ardèche

1 Major Site in Aven d'Orgnac, the Cave

A cave with stupefying volumes that opens up a mythical wonderland: draperies, piles of plates, giant palm trees. A sound and light show enhances the site 121 metres underground before an effortless return to ground level by lift.
http://www.orgnac.com/

2 Major site in Aven d'Orgnac, Cité de la Préhistoire

A voyage through 350,000 years of prehistory, made interactive and fun by realistic sounds, learning visuals and multi-player touch tables. The best way to take a fresh view of archaelogy.
http://www.orgnac.com

3 Musée de Soyons

With its 150,000 years of history, the Soyons site is an important testimony to the main phases of the human adventure. The guided visit of the caves and the museum plunges the visitor into the fascinating universe of prehistory and history.
http://www.soyons.fr/

4 Grotte de Saint-Marcel

A listed site since 1934, the cave is famous for its gours and calcite basins filled with water. A journey back in time, prolonged by a discovery trail in the forest, the *Chemin de la Grosse Pierre*.
http://www.grotte-st-marcel.com

5 Aven Marzal

This site is unique in Europe, combining a magnificent cave, a free-access museum with a rich collection on the underground world, and a zoo called "The Dino Forest".
http://www.aven-marzal.com

6 Grotte de la Madeleine

The Madeleine cave is one of the most astounding natural formations sculpted by groundwater, and their beauty is magnified by a sound and light show. In addition, the Madeleine belvedere offers an extraordinary panorama of the gorges of the Ardèche River.
http://www.grottemadeleine.com

7 Chauvet Cave Exhibition at Vallon-Pont d'Arc

The exhibition takes us into the incomparable atmosphere of the Chauvet-Pont d'Arc Cave to discover the world's oldest prehistoric paintings. Stuffed animals, photographs, displays, an exclusive film about the discoverers, and games all contribute to a greater understanding of a site unique in the world.
http://www.prehistoireardeche.com

8 Alba-la-Romaine

The museum that prolongs the historic site of Alba-la-Romaine offers an opportunity to discover the many objects uncovered by recent archaeological excavations and a 3D model reproducing part of the ancient city.
http://www.ardeche.fr

9 La Caverne du Pont-d'Arc

The first of its kind, the cultural and scientific project of the Pont d'Arc Cavern is an exact replica of the original cave built on the site of Razal overlooking Vallon-Pont d'Arc. It reproduces the beauty and wonder of the drawings and paintings created 36,000 years ago by Aurignacian artists. Opens in 2015.
www.lacavernedupontdarc.org

Passerelles Patrimoines

A network of professionals who offer activities combining nature and culture all year round.
www.passerelles-patrimoines-ardeche.com

Source: Agence de développement touristique de l'Ardèche.

Chauvet-Pont d'Arc in dates and in numbers

-36,000 years

First passage of humans (Aurignacians) and decoration of the cave.

-30,000 years

Second passage of humans (Gravettians) presumably with no contribution to the artworks.

-21,500 years

Collapse of the overhang that permanently closed off the entrance to the cavity.

1994

The cave's discovery by Jean-Marie Chauvet, Éliette Brunel and Christian Hillaire.

1995

Announcement of the cavity's discovery and listing as a French Historical Monument.

1997

Acquisition of the cavity by the French state and the first preservation measures.

1998

Beginning of the scientific study of the cavity.

2007

Launching of the project for the cavity's Reproduction Space.

2012

Placing the "first hand" on the Reproduction Space.

2014

Listed as a UNESCO World Heritage Site.

2015

Opening of the Chauvet-Pont d'Arc Cave replica, under the name of "Pont-d'Arc Cavern".

N 44° 23' 15" - E 04° 24' 58"

Latitude and longitude of the Chauvet-Pont d'Arc Cave.

200 metres

Altitude of the Chauvet-Pont d'Arc Cave.

13.5 °C

Mean temperature in the first section of the cavity.

12 °C

Mean temperature at the bottom of the cavity.

99.5 %

Humidity in the cavity.

442

Number of animals depicted on the walls.

1,000

Approximate number of figures represented.

242 metres

Total length of the cavity.

8,500 square metres

Total surface area of the cave.

16 billion

Number of points recorded for the 3D model.

51 million euros

Budget for the Pont-d'Arc Cavern replica.

1,200 tonnes

Total mass of the Pont-d'Arc Cavern.

100 km

Total length of the metal rods assembled to reproduce the volumes of the Pont-d'Arc Cavern.

Present and Past Members of the Chauvet-Pont d'Arc Cave Scientific Team

DIRECTORS

Jean Clottes (1998—2002) and Jean-Michel Geneste

PRESENT TEAM

• Cave Art and Archaeology

Marc Azéma, Dominique Baffier, Elisa Boche, Jean Clottes, Valérie Feruglio, Philippe Fosse, Carole Fritz, Bernard Gély, Jean-Michel Geneste, Frédéric Maksud, Julien Monney, Gilles Tosello

• Environmental Studies

Jean-Jacques Delannoy, Stéphane Jaillet, Estelle Ployon, Benjamin Sadier: karstology

Catherine Ferrier, Bertrand Kervazo, Stéphane Konik, Dominique Lafon, Evelyne Debard: sedimentology

Dominique Genty: speleothems

Isabelle Théry, Stéphanie Thiébault: anthracology

• Specific Analysis

Jean-Marc Elalouf: DNA

Céline Bon: DNA

Michel Girard: palynology

Yanik Le Guillou: cave art

Michel Menu: pigments

Michel Philippe: palaeontology

Hugues Plisson: flint tool microtraces

Hélène Valladas, Anita Quilès: ^{14}C dating

Pierre Guibert: dating

PAST MEMBERS

Maurice Arnold: dating

Norbert Aujoulat: cave art specialist (deceased)

Jacques Evin: dating (deceased)

Michel-Alain Garcia: ichnologist (deceased)

Claude Guérin: palaeontologist

Philippe Morel: palaeontologist (deceased)

Christine Oberlin: dating

Craig Packer: ethologist

Yves Perrette: karstologist

Joëlle Robert-Lamblin: anthropologist

François Rouzaud: topographer and speleologist (deceased)

Jean-Louis Schefer: art historian

Nadine Tisnerat: dating

Hervé Bocherens: biochemical studies

Chauvet-Pont d'Arc cave Scientific Committee – Unesco Candidature and Reproduction Space

PRESIDENT

Jean Clottes – General Curator of Cultural Heritage in France (Honorary), international rock art specialist for UNESCO and ICOMOS and Honorary President of the French Prehistoric Society

MEMBERS

Marie Bardisa – Curator of the Chauvet-Pont d'Arc Cave

Jean-Michel Geneste – Director of the Scientific Team of the Chauvet-Pont d'Arc Cave and Honorary Director of the French National Prehistory Centre

Jean-Jacques Delannoy – Director, EDYTEM Laboratory, University of Savoy, France

Geneviève Pinçon – Scientific Adviser, Roc-aux-Sorciers Site

Gerhard Bosinski – Honorary Professor, University of Cologne

Roberto Ontañón Peredo – Chief, Archaeology Section, Cultural Heritage Service, Cantabria Province, Spain

Marc Groenen – Professor of Prehistory, Free University of Brussels

Harald Floss – Prehistorian, University of Tübingen

André Delpuech – Chief Curator, Quai Branly Museum, Paris

Abdellah Salih – Director, Cultural Heritage of Morocco

Margaret Conkey – Professor of Anthropology, University of California, Berkeley

Yann-Pierre Montelle – Prehistorian, University of Canterbury, New Zealand

Miquel Barcelo – Plastic Artist

Anne Lebot-Helly – Chief, Regional Archaeology Service, DRAC Rhône-Alpes, France

Patricia Guillermin – Curator, Regional Museum of Archaeology, Orgnac-l'Aven, Ardèche, France

Companies in charge of the Cavern's construction

CONTRACTING AUTHORITY

Pont-d'Arc Cavern Joint Association

ARCHITECTURAL TEAM

Architect: *Fabre Speller*

Associate Architect: *Atelier 3A*

Technical Engineering All Works: *Girus*

Technical Engineering Economy: *Girus*

Scenography: *Scène*

Landscape Gardener: *Franck Neau*

Organisation, Planning and Coordination: *Global*

Inspection Body: *Socotec*

Health, Prevention and Safety Coordination: *01-Excor*

Fire Safety System Coordination: *Girus*

FACSIMILE, SCENOGRAPHY, SCULPTURES AND PAINTINGS

Socra-Campenon Bernard Régions (Vinci Construction Group France): Technical and Artistic Direction – Control and Coordination – Exploitation of the 3D Model – Synthesis – Design of Construction Tools

Freyssinet, Cofex, AAB: Metal Structures – Geological Facies Sculptures – Integration of Works Produced in the Ateliers – Ichnology

Phénomènes: Creation of Speleothems – Calcite on Rocks

Cossima Productions-Dasplet: Creation of Skeletal Remains

Arc et Os, Création Graphique, Déco Diffusion: Creation of Decorated Panels

Perazio Engineering: Creation of the Anamorphic 3D Digital Model

COMPANIES

Earthworks: *Laurans - Chandolas*, Co-contractor: *Satp Sacer*

Shell: *Berthouly*, Co-contractors: *Rivasi BTP / Mima Charmasson*

Metal Frame Structure: *Cabrol*

Wooden Frame Structure: *Moulin Charpente*

Plumbing and Sanitation: *Fourel*

Heating and Ventilation: *Chaussabel*

Electricity: *Sneff*

Roofing and Waterproofing: *Smac*

External Joinery: *Zancanaro*

Metalworking: *Giraud Delay - Alissas*, Co-contractor: *Andriollo*

Internal Joinery: *Gero*, Co-contractor: *Chazalon*

Hard Floor Covering: *Faïences Sportiello*

BIBLIOGRAPHY

Préhistoire de l'art occidental, André Leroi-Gourhan, Éditions Mazenod, 1965.

La Grotte Chauvet à Vallon-Pont-d'Arc, Jean-Marie Chauvet, Éliette Brunel-Deschamps et Christian Hillaire, Postface de Jean Clottes, Éditions du Seuil, 1995.

Les Chamanes de la Préhistoire. Transe et magie dans les grottes ornées, Jean Clottes et David Lewis-Williams, Éditions du Seuil, 1996.

Grottes ornées de l'Ardèche, l'art des cavernes, Bernard Gély, Éditions Le Dauphiné Libéré, coll. Les Patrimoines, 2000.

Les Gorges de l'Ardèche, une réserve naturelle, Collectif, Éditions Le Dauphiné Libéré, coll. Les Patrimoines, 2002.

Les Félins de la grotte Chauvet, Jean Clottes et Marc Azéma, Éditions du Seuil, coll. Les cahiers de la grotte Chauvet, 2005.

Les Mammouths de la grotte Chauvet, Bernard Gély et Marc Azéma, Éditions du Seuil, coll. Les cahiers de la grotte Chauvet, 2005.

"La Grotte Chauvet : conservation d'un patrimoine", Dominique Baffier, *Bulletin de la Société préhistorique française (Karstologia Mémoires)*, 2005, tome 102, n° 1, pp. 11-16.

"La Grotte Chauvet à Vallon-Pont-d'Arc (Ardèche). Le contexte régional paléolithique", Bernard Gély, *Bulletin de la Société préhistorique française (Karstologia Mémoires)*, 2005, tome 102, n° 1, pp. 17-33.

"Ichnologie générale de la grotte Chauvet", Michel-Alain Garcia, *Bulletin de la Société préhistorique française (Karstologia Mémoires)*, 2005, tome 102, n° 1, pp. 103-108.

"Bilan des datations carbone 14 effectuées sur des charbons de bois de la grotte Chauvet", Hélène Valladas, Nadine Tisnérat-Laborde, Hélène Cacher, Évelyne Kaltnecker, Maurice Arnold, Christine Oberlin, Jacques Evin, *Bulletin de la Société préhistorique française (Karstologia Mémoires)*, 2005, tome 102, n° 1, pp. 109-113.

"Les images des félins de la grotte Chauvet", Jean Clottes et Marc Azéma, *Bulletin de la Société préhistorique française (Karstologia Mémoires)*, 2005, tome 102, n° 1, pp. 173-182.

"Contribution de la saisie tridimensionnelle à l'étude de l'art pariétal et de son contexte physique", Norbert Aujoulat, Guy Perazio, David Faverge, José-Francisco Peral, *Bulletin de la Société préhistorique française, (Karstologia Mémoires)*, 2005, tome 102, n° 1, pp. 189-197.

"La symbolique de la grotte Chauvet-Pont d'Arc sous le regard de l'anthropologie", Joëlle Robert-Lamblin, *Bulletin de la Société préhistorique française (Karstologia Mémoires)*, 2005, tome 102, n° 1, pp. 199-208.

"De la faune au bestiaire - La grotte Chauvet-Pont-d'Arc, aux origines de l'art pariétal paléolithique", Valérie Feruglio, *Comptes-rendus Palevol*, n° 5, 2006, pp. 213-222.

"Deciphering the Complete Mitochondrial Genome and Phylogeny of the Extinct Cave Bear in the Paleolithic Painted Cave of Chauvet", Bon *et al.*, *PNAS*, 2008, vol. 105, pp. 17447-17452.

"Un art très ancien en Roumanie. Les dates de Coliboaia", Jean Clottes, Bernard Gély, Calin Ghemis, Évelyne Kaltnecker, Viorel Traian Lascu, *Inora (International Newsletter on Rock Art)*, n° 61, 2011.

Pourquoi l'art préhistorique ?, Jean Clottes, Éditions Gallimard, 2011.

La Préhistoire du cinéma : Origines paléolithiques de la narration graphique et du cinématographe..., Marc Azéma, Éditions Errance, 2011.

"Low Regional Diversity of Late Cave Bears Mitochondrial DNA at the Time of Chauvet Aurignacian Paintings", Bon *et al.*, *Journal of Archaeological Science*, 2011, vol. 38, pp. 1886-1895.

"L'Europe de la culture est née il y a trente-six mille ans", Pedro Lima, *Revue des deux mondes*, n° 4, 2012.

"Further Constraints on the Chauvet Cave Artwork Elaboration", Benjamin Sadier et *al.*, *Proceedings of the National Academy of Science of the USA*, 2012, tome 109, n° 21, pp. 8002 - 8006.

"L'art paléolithique de la Baume Latrone (France, Gard) : nouveaux éléments de datation", Marc Azéma, Bernard Gély, Raphaëlle Bourrillon, Philippe Galant, *Inora (International Newsletter on Rock Art)*, n° 64, 2012.

"Les Aménagements et structures anthropiques de la grotte Chauvet-Pont d'Arc. Apport d'une approche intégrative géomorpho-archéologique", Jean-Jacques Delannoy, Jean-Michel Geneste, Stéphane Jaillet, Élisa Boche, Benjamin Sadier, Karsts, *Paysages et Préhistoire*, coll. Edytem, n° 13, 2012.

"Animation in Palaeolithic Art: a Pre-Echo of Cinema", Marc Azéma et Florent Rivère, *Antiquity*, 2012, vol. 86, n° 332, pp 316-324.

"L'ours spéléologue", Jean-Marc Elalouf et Valérie Feruglio, *Pour la Science*, n° 412, 2012.

La Grotte Chauvet-Pont d'Arc, sanctuaire préhistorique, Jean Clottes, Éditions Le Dauphiné Libéré, coll. Les Patrimoines, 2013.

"Rendre à la lumière les premières images de l'humanité : Espace de restitution la Caverne du Pont-d'Arc - Ardèche", Richard Buffat, *Inora (International Newsletter on Rock Art)*, n° 69, 2014.

Official page of the Chauvet-Pont d'Arc cave on the website of the French Ministry of Culture: *http://www.culture.gouv.fr/fr/arcnat/chauvet/fr*

PHOTOGRAPHIC CREDITS

All the photographs illustrating this work are by Philippe Psaïla, except those mentioned below.

Page 34: Javier Trueba /MSF/ SPL

Page 35: Yvonne Mühleis © Landesamt für Denkmalpflege im RP Stuttgart/Ulmer Museum

Pages 40 - 41, 42 - 43, 45, 46, 48, 50, 51, 52 - 53: Stéphane Jaillet / Edytem

Page 43: Fayolle/Sipa

Pages 44, 48: DRAC Rhône-Alpes

Page 47: Pascal Goetgheluck

Pages 58-59: Cabinet Perazio

Page 62: Benjamin Sadier / Edytem

Pages 172-173: Serge Valcke / Cabinet Perazio

Page 194: Fabre-Speller

The images taken from the 3D model were made by Philippe Psaïla, in collaboration with the *Cabinet Perazio.*

Acknowledgements

The author wishes above all to thank the three discoverers of the Chauvet-Pont d'Arc cave: Éliette Brunel, Jean-Marie Chauvet and Christian Hillaire who allowed us to rediscover, 36,000 years after its creation, the first masterpiece of our shared humanity, delivering it intact to the world thanks to their immediate efforts to protect it.

He is also grateful to Aurélie Filippetti, France's Minister of Culture and Communication for writing the preface to this work and to Pascal Terrasse, President of the *Syndicat mixte de la Caverne du Pont-d'Arc* for giving the necessary impetus to this book. His warmest thanks go to Marie Bardisa, Curator of the Chauvet-Pont d'Arc cave for offering him the opportunity to experience firsthand the matchless emotion stirred by these paintings.

Specials thanks go to Guy Perazio, who created the 3D model of the original cavity and the Anamorphosis for the *Syndicat mixte*, and to his entire team, particularly Serge Valcke, José-Francisco Peral, Benjamin Sadier and Lionel Guichard for sharing this extraordinary tool, admirably put to use by Philippe Psaïla to illustrate the present work, as well as Stéphane Jaillet for his assistance with the iconography.

He also thanks Richard Buffat and Sébastien Gayet of the *Syndicat mixte de la Caverne du Pont-d'Arc* for their contribution to the writing of this book, as well as Fidèle Sola of *Campenon Bernard Régions* for her valuable help.

A special debt of gratitude goes to Benjamin Sadier for his vigilant and open-minded scientific advice, and to Jean Clottes, so intimately linked to the history of this cavity, who communicated his passion back in 1995, as well as to Dominique Baffier and Valérie Feruglio, who have always been generous in sharing their knowledge. Thanks also go to Jean-Michel Geneste for his attentive reading of the French manuscript and to Yann-Pierre Montelle for bringing his linguistic expertise to the English translation.

He owes thanks to Anaïs Psaïla, Marion Enguehard and Venetia Bell, who have respectively designed the book, reread the texts and translated them into English with equal precision and sensitivity.

And last but not least, thanks to our Aurignacian ancestors, the genial creators of these unforgettable works, the first artists and wholly *Homo sapiens*, for having opened up the way.

Chauvet-Pont d'Arc

THE FIRST MASTERPIECE OF HUMANITY

REVEALED BY 3D

Text by Pedro Lima
Photographs and multimedia by Philippe Psaïla
3D Images by Philippe Psaïla and Cabinet Perazio
Preface: Aurélie Filippetti
Forward: Pascal Terrasse
Scientific Adviser: Benjamin Sadier
Translation by Venetia Bell
Book design and illustrations: Anaïs Psaïla
Correction and revision of the French manuscript: Marion Enguehard
Conception and coordination: Philippe Psaïla

Published in France under the title
Chauvet-Pont d'Arc
Le premier chef-d'œuvre de l'humanité révélé par la 3D
Printed in Belgium in July 2014

by Cassochrome for
Éditions SYNOPS
10 rue des Belges, 26200 Montélimar, France
www.synops-editions.fr/

Dépôt légal Bibliothèque Nationale de France: July 2014
ISBN: 978-2-9542888-3-3

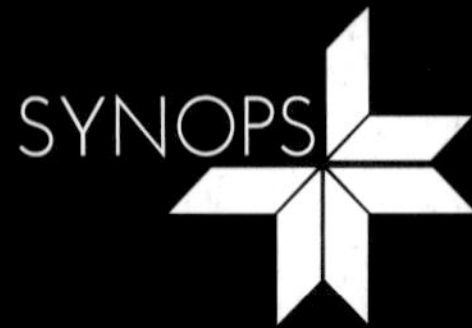

"This product is from sustainably managed forests and controlled sources using 100% renewable energy."

This work is published in partnership with the Ardèche General Council, the Rhône-Alpes Region and the Pont d'Arc Cavern Joint Syndicate.